SEP 2 6 2011

D0858493

Japanese for All Occasions

Japanese for All Occasions

Mastering Speech Styles from Casual to Honorific

TAEKO KAMIYA

KODANSHA INTERNATIONAL
Tokyo • New York • London

Sections marked with this icon are available as audio on the attached CD.

Narration by Reiko Matsunaga, Aiko Nakajima, Yoshiki Oneda, Ikuko Sawada, Takatoshi Takeda, and Tatsuhiro Nishinosono, through arrangement with PSC Produce and Management.
Child's voice by Itsuki Kurokawa.
CD recording and editing by The English Language Education Council Inc.
Illustrations by Osamu Hayakawa.
Editorial assistance & book design by guild.

Distributed in the United States by Kodansha America, LLC, and in the United Kingdom and continental Europe by Kodansha Europe Ltd.

Published by Kodansha International Ltd., 17-14 Otowa 1-chome, Bunkyo-ku, Tokyo 112-8652.

First edition, 2010
20 19 18 17 16 15 14 13 12 11 10   10 9 8 7 6 5 4 3 2 1

Library of Congress Cataloging-in-Publication Data

Kamiya, Taeko.
Japanese for all occasions : mastering speech styles from casual to honorific /
  Taeko Kamiya. — 1st ed.
    p. cm.
  Includes bibliographical references.
  ISBN 978-4-7700-3151-8
  1. Japanese language—Conversation and phrase books—English. 2.
Japanese language—Spoken Japanese. I. Title.
PL539.K246 2010
495.6'83421—dc22

                         2010038375

CONTENTS

APPENDIXES

Do you wish to speak Japanese as the Japanese do? If your answer is yes, then you will have to learn speech styles. From casual to honorific, each style has its own level of politeness. The use of speech styles is one of the most challenging aspects of Japanese; and yet without some understanding of it, it is easy to come off in conversation as too familiar or too distant.

Imagine you are speaking to a social superior, such as your boss or a professor. Naturally you will need to use polite language. On the other hand, say you are talking with a close friend—if you don't speak in a casual style, you will sound cold to him.

In Japanese, there are virtually unlimited ways to express a single sentence. Take the pronoun "I," for instance: in polite conversation it is *watashi*, in formal conversation it is *watakushi*, and in casual conversation by a male speaker it is *boku*. In casual conversation by a female speaker, it is again *watashi*. "Where are you going?" can be translated into Japanese as *Doko e ikimasu ka* in the polite style, *Doko e iku* in the plain (casual) style, and *Dochira e irasshaimasu ka* in the honorific style.

The primary purpose of this book is to help you understand how Japanese conversation is carried out in different social settings, and to teach you some of the basic rules for each style so that you can apply them to your own speech. Its secondary purpose is to introduce some of the most frequently used sentence patterns encountered at the intermediate level of study, which is when students begin to study honorifics.

The book is divided into two parts. Part I deals with how Japanese words and sentences are formed in different speech styles. Part II—consisting of nineteen lessons—presents various scenes where conversation is carried out in (A) the polite style between/among adults who are not close friends, (B) the plain (casual) style between/among family members and close friends, and (C) the honorific/humble style between/among people of different social statuses, or when talking about someone of a higher status than oneself. Practice questions are provided at the end of each lesson to allow you to test your understanding.

I hope that this book will prove helpful, that you will grasp some of the basic rules for different speech styles and learn to better communicate with Japanese people.

Taeko Kamiya
Pacific Grove, California

List of Abbreviations

Adj = adjective

Adj stem = stem of an adjective, e.g. 寒 of 寒い (cold); 静か of 静かな (quiet)

N = noun

S = sentence ending in the plain style (with either a verb or an i-adjective, or with a na-adjective/noun followed by だ / だった)

Vdic = dictionary form of a verb

Vneg = negative stem of a verb, e.g. 書か of 書かない (not write); 見せ of 見せない (not show); 来 of 来ない (not come); し of しない (not do)

Vstem = -ます stem of a verb, e.g. 歩き of 歩きます (walk); 開け of 開けます (open); 来 of 来ます (come); し of します (do)

Vta = -た form of a verb, e.g. 飲んだ (drank); 覚えた (memorized); 来た (came); した (did)

Vtara = -たら form of a verb, e.g. 買ったら (if/when [you] buy); できたら (if/when [you] can); 来たら (if/when [you] come); したら (if/when [you] do)

Vtari = -たり form of a verb, e.g. 話したり (sometimes [I] speak); 答えたり (sometimes [I] answer); 来たり (sometimes [I] come); したり (sometimes [I] do)

Vte = -て form of a verb, e.g. 書いて (write and …); 調べて (check and …); 来て (come and …); して (do and …)

Vvol = plain volitional form of a verb, e.g. 行こう (let's go); 見よう (let's see); 来よう (let's come); しよう (let's do)

BASIC FORMATION

The Japanese language has four basic styles of speech: plain, polite, honorific, and humble. The plain style is used in conversation among family and close friends, as well as in fiction, nonfiction, professional journals, and official documents. The polite style is used in conversation among adults who are not close friends, and in letters, children's books, and some adult books. The honorific style is employed when you address or refer to your superior—someone who is older or higher in social standing than yourself. The humble style is preferred when you talk to your superior about yourself or someone close to you. This section deals with how personal pronouns, names, nouns, adjectives, and verbs are formed in the different speech styles.

PERSONAL PRONOUNS

There is a large variety of personal pronouns in Japanese. Different words are used depending on the formality of the situation or the gender of the speaker.

Singular Personal Pronouns

	First Person (I)	Second Person (you)
Superpolite	私 （わたくし）	—
Polite	私 （わたし）	あなた
Plain	僕 * （ぼく）	君 （きみ）
Rough	おれ *	お前 * （まえ）

* used by male speakers

Plural Personal Pronouns

	First Person (we)	Second Person (you)
Superpolite	私共 （わたくしども）	—
Polite	私達 （わたくしたち）	あなた方 （がた）
Plain	私達 （わたしたち） 僕達 / 僕ら * （ぼくたち）（ぼく）	あなた達 （たち） 君達 / 君ら * （きみたち）（きみ）
Rough	おれ達 / おれら * （たち）	お前達 / お前ら * （まえたち）（まえ）

* used by male speakers   ** 彼（かれ） cannot take -達（たち）

NOTES

1. Personal pronouns, especially first- and second-person pronouns, are often omitted if the meaning of the sentence is clear without them.

2. この人 / この方 (this person), その人 / その方 (that person right there), and あの人 / あの方 (that person over there) are often used for "he/she." 彼 (he) or 彼女 (she) may be used as well, but be aware that these words can also mean "boyfriend" or "girlfriend."

3. The demonstrative pronouns こちら, そちら, あちら, and どちら are interchangeable with この方, その方, あの方, and どの方. Likewise, これ, それ, あれ, and どれ are interchangeable with この人, その人, あの人, and どの人.

Third Person (he/she)	Interrogative (who/which)
—	—
こちら / そちら / あちら この方 / その方 / あの方	どなた どの方 / どちら
彼 / 彼女 これ / それ / あれ この人 / その人 / あの人	だれ どの人 / どれ
—	—

Third Person (they)	Interrogative (which ones)
—	—
この方々 / その方々 / あの方々	どの方々
彼女達 / 彼ら ** この人達 / その人達 / あの人達	どの人達
—	—

NAMES

Japanese is different from English in the way people address or refer to one another. First, there are a number of different courtesy titles, some of which do not translate into English. Second, Japanese people frequently use job titles not only to refer to others but also to address them. And finally, there are separate words for "mother," "father," "brother," "sister,"

Courtesy Titles

Title	Usage
-さん	**(1)** *Mr., Mrs., Ms.* May be attached to a person's family name, given name, or full name. In Japanese, the family name precedes the given name. In most cases, Japanese people prefer to address one another by family name plus -さん. They usually do not call each other by given names unless they are very close. (2) May be used with certain occupations.
-様	*Mr., Mrs., Ms.* Is politer than -さん. Hotel staff and store clerks commonly use -様 with a family name to address a customer. -様 is also used with a full name to write an address on an envelope.
-氏	*Mr., Mrs., Ms.* Is used to refer to a professional person or public figure, particularly in writing. Is not used to address people.
-君	*Does not translate into English.* Comes after a family name or given name. Used to be used only by boys and men to address male friends. Nowadays girls use it too. Teachers—male or female—use -君 after a family name to address male students.
-ちゃん	*Does not translate into English.* Comes after a given name. Is used affectionately to address or refer to children and old friends from childhood.

and other family members, the choice of which depends on whether one is referring to one's own family or to someone else's.

Names and Courtesy Titles

Japanese people address or refer to others with various courtesy titles as shown in the chart below. The titles come after the name. None of them should be used with one's own name or with the names of one's family members.

Examples	
(1) 田中さん	Mr./Mrs./Ms. Tanaka
正夫さん	Masao (male given name)
和子さん	Kazuko (female given name)
田中正夫さん	Mr. Masao Tanaka
田中和子さん	Mrs./Ms. Kazuko Tanaka
(2) 運転手さん	driver
肉屋さん	butcher
看護師さん	nurse
吉田様	Mr./Mrs./Ms. Yoshida
吉田幸子様	Mrs./Ms./Miss Sachiko Yoshida
原田氏	Mr./Mrs./Ms. Harada
原田孝雄氏	Mr. Takao Harada
山野君	Yamano (family name)
明君	Akira (male given name)
孝ちゃん	Takashi (male given name)
広子ちゃん	Hiroko (female given name)

Names and Job Titles

To address or refer to persons of a certain occupation, it is common to use their job titles (with or without their names).

（<ruby>和田<rt>わ だ</rt></ruby>）<ruby>課長<rt>か ちょう</rt></ruby>   Section Chief (Wada)

（<ruby>岡<rt>おか</rt></ruby>）<ruby>部長<rt>ぶ ちょう</rt></ruby>   General Manager (Oka)

（<ruby>本田<rt>ほん だ</rt></ruby>）<ruby>社長<rt>しゃちょう</rt></ruby>   Company President (Honda)

（<ruby>石田<rt>いし だ</rt></ruby>）<ruby>知事<rt>ち じ</rt></ruby>   Governor (Ishida)

（<ruby>木田<rt>き だ</rt></ruby>）<ruby>市長<rt>し ちょう</rt></ruby>   Mayor (Kida)

（<ruby>矢野<rt>や の</rt></ruby>）<ruby>先生<rt>せんせい</rt></ruby>   Professor (Yano)

<ruby>先生<rt>せんせい</rt></ruby> is a courtesy title that may be used with or in place of the names of doctors, lawyers, writers, Diet members, etc.

Note that Japanese usually avoid using the second-person pronoun あなた when addressing superiors or others of higher social standing than themselves. Instead, they use the person's name or job title.

1. <ruby>岸<rt>きし</rt></ruby>さんはあのクラブの<ruby>会員<rt>かいいん</rt></ruby>ですか。

   Are you (Mr. Kishi) a member of that club? (Mr. Kishi is an older neighbor)

2. <ruby>課長<rt>か ちょう</rt></ruby>は<ruby>東大学<rt>ひがしだいがく</rt></ruby>のご<ruby>出身<rt>しゅっしん</rt></ruby>ですか。

   Are you (Section Chief) a graduate of Higashi University? (the section chief is your boss)

Words for Family Members

The terms used to address or refer to family members or relatives are provided in two distinct sets, as shown in the following chart.

Family Members

	Referential Terms		Address Terms	
	One's Own	Someone Else's	One's Own	Someone Else's
Father	父 （ちち）	お父 （とう）さん / お父 （とう）様 （さま）	お父 （とう）さん	お父 （とう）さん / お父 （とう）様 （さま）
Mother	母 （はは）	お母 （かあ）さん / お母 （かあ）様 （さま）	お母 （かあ）さん	お母 （かあ）さん / お母 （かあ）様 （さま）
Older Brother	兄 （あに）	お兄 （にい）さん / お兄 （にい）様 （さま）	お兄 （にい）さん	given name ＋さん
Younger Brother	弟 （おとうと）	弟 （おとうと）さん	given name	given name ＋ ちゃん / くん / さん
Older Sister	姉 （あね）	お姉 （ねえ）さん / お姉 （ねえ）様 （さま）	お姉 （ねえ）さん	given name ＋ さん
Younger Sister	妹 （いもうと）	妹 （いもうと）さん	given name	given name ＋ ちゃん / くん / さん
Son	息子 （むすこ）	息子 （むすこ）さん	given name	given name ＋ くん / さん
Daughter	娘 （むすめ）	娘 （むすめ）さん	given name	given name ＋ ちゃん / さん
Child	子供 （こども） 子 （こ）	子供 （こども）さん / お子 （こ）さん	given name	given name ＋ ちゃん / くん
Grandfather	祖父 （そふ）	おじいさん / おじい様 （さま）	おじいさん	おじいさん / おじい様 （さま）
Grandmother	祖母 （そぼ）	おばあさん / おばあ様 （さま）	おばあさん	おばあさん / おばあ様 （さま）
Uncle	おじ	おじさん / おじ様 （さま）	おじさん	おじさん / おじ様 （さま）
Aunt	おば	おばさん / おば様 （さま）	おばさん	おばさん / おば様 （さま）
Husband	主人 （しゅじん）	ご主人 （しゅじん） / ご主人様 （しゅじんさま）	あなた given name	family/given name ＋さん
Wife	家内 （かない） 妻 （つま）	奥 （おく）さん / 奥様 （おくさま）	given name	奥 （おく）さん / 奥様 （おくさま） given name ＋ さん
Parents	両親 （りょうしん）	ご両親 （りょうしん）	—	—
Family	家族 （かぞく）	ご家族 （かぞく）	—	—

HONORIFIC PREFIXES お- AND ご-

The honorific prefixes お- and ご- are used with nouns and adjectives. There are two usages. The first is when one is talking about the things, actions, or states of social superiors. Basically, お- is used for Japanese-origin words (*kun*-reading words) and ご- for Chinese-origin words (*on*-reading words).

Nouns

(a) Japanese-origin words: お体〈からだ〉   body
                        お仕事〈しごと〉   work

                        おひま   free time

(b) Chinese-origin words: ご住所〈じゅうしょ〉 address
                        ご意見〈いけん〉   opinion
                        ご到着〈とうちゃく〉 arrival

     Some Chinese-origin words take お- or both お- and ご-: お電話〈でんわ〉 (telephone), お時間〈じかん〉 (time), お料理〈りょうり〉 (cooking), お返事〈へんじ〉 / ご返事〈へんじ〉 (reply).

1. お仕事〈しごと〉はいかがですか。

How is work?

2. ここにご住所〈じゅうしょ〉をお書〈か〉きください。

Please write your address here.

3. 鈴木〈すずき〉さんがお電話〈でんわ〉をくださいました。

Mr. Suzuki called me.

Adjectives

(a) Japanese-origin words (all i-adjectives and some na-adjectives):

お忙〈いそが〉しい	busy	お静〈しず〉かな	quiet
お若〈わか〉い	young	お好〈す〉きな	favorite

(b) Chinese-origin words (na-adjectives only):

ご親切な　　kind
ご丁寧な　　polite
ご立派な　　magnificent

Some Chinese-origin words take お-: お上手な (skillful), お元気な (healthy).

1. 小田先生はいつもお忙しいです。

Professor Oda is always busy.

2. お好きなお飲み物は何ですか。

What is your favorite drink?

3. お母様はお元気ですか。

Is your mother well?

4. 社長はゴルフがお上手ですね。

Our (company) president is good at golf, isn't he?

The second usage of お- and ご- is for politeness. お- and ご- can be attached to things, actions, or states that are not related to one's superiors but are part of one's daily life, to make one's speech sound more elegant. Women tend to use お- and ご- in this way more often than men. One should avoid using these prefixes excessively.

Nouns		**Adjectives**	
お菓子	sweets	お暑い	hot
お茶	tea	お寒い	cold
お手洗い	bathroom	お静かな	quiet
お休み	vacation		

5

1. 毎日（まいにち）お寒（さむ）いですね。

It's cold day after day, isn't it?

2. 明日（あした）はお休（やす）みだから朝寝坊（あさねぼう）します。

Tomorrow is a holiday, so I won't be getting up early.

3. このお菓子（かし）、おいしそうね。

This cake looks delicious, doesn't it?

4. 今日（きょう）はピアノのおけいこがあるの。

I have a piano lesson today.

Note that お- and ご- cannot be used with foreign words, public facilities, or words that start with お.

(a) Foreign words:	ビール	beer
	コーヒー	coffee
	バター	butter
	テーブル	table
	ドア	door
	エレベーター	elevator
(b) Public facilities:	学校（がっこう）	school
	図書館（としょかん）	library
	公園（こうえん）	park
(c) Words that start with お:	おばさん	aunt
	おび	obi, sash for a kimono
	おいしい	delicious
	おもしろい	interesting

COPULAS (BE-VERBS)

The Japanese copulas だ, です, and でございます are equivalent to "am," "is," or "are." When they follow a noun, they act as the predicate verb of the sentence. だ is used for the plain style, です for the polite style, and でございます for the superpolite style—which can be honorific, humble, or just polite depending on the subject of the sentence. The various forms of the copula are shown in the chart below.

Copulas

	Plain	Polite	Superpolite
Present (is, am, are)	だ	です	でございます
Negative (is/am/are not)	で (は) ない	で (は) ありません	で (は) ございません
Past (was, were)	だった	でした	でございました
Negative Past (was/were not)	で (は) なかった	で (は) ありません でした	で (は) ございません でした
Presumptive (probably)	だろう	でしょう	でございましょう
Conditional (if)	なら / だったら	でしたら	でございましたら

Copulas have two basic usages. The first is as a predicate verb in the "A is B" construction.

1. 彼は兄の友達だ。 (plain)

He is my older brother's friend.

2. 山中さんは学校の先生です。 (polite)

Ms. Yamanaka is a schoolteacher.

3. あの方が森田社長でございます。 (honorific)

That man is Mr. Morita, president of the company.

4. 父は判事でございました。 (humble)

My father was a judge.

5. あれは中央郵便局でございます。 (superpolite)

That is the Central Post Office.

6. 雨なら / でしたら試合はございません。 (superpolite)

If it rains, there will be no game.

The second usage is as a substitute for other verbs (when the meaning is clear from the context).

1. 僕はステーキだ (= にする)。 (plain)

I'll have steak.

2. 映画は3時からです (= 始まります)。 (polite)

The movie starts at three o'clock.

3. 林先生は会議室でございます (= にいらっしゃいます)。

Professor Hayashi is in the conference room. (honorific)

4. レストランは3階でございます (= にございます)。

The restaurant is located on the third floor. (superpolite)

ADJECTIVES

Japanese adjectives come in two types: i-adjectives that end in
い, and na-adjectives that end in な. When used as predicates, i-
adjectives behave like verbs, while na-adjectives behave like nouns.
Both have plain, polite, and superpolite styles.

I-adjectives

For the plain style of i-adjectives, the dictionary form (present form)
and its conjugated forms (negative, past, and negative past) are used.
For the polite style, the copula です is added to the end of the adjective. And for the superpolite style, the stems undergo some changes
before ございます as shown on the next page.

寒い Cold

	Plain	Polite	Superpolite
Present (is cold)	寒い	寒いです	(お)寒う ございます
Negative (is not cold)	寒くない	寒くないです	(お)寒う ございません
Past (was cold)	寒かった	寒かったです	(お)寒う ございました
Negative Past (was not cold)	寒くなかった	寒くなかったです	(お)寒うござい ませんでした
Presumptive (is probably cold)	寒いだろう	寒いでしょう	(お)寒う ございましょう
Conditional (if it is cold)	寒ければ / 寒かったら	—	(お)寒う ございましたら

The stems of i-adjectives change as follows before ございます in
the superpolite style:

(a) ai → ō   nagai   →   nagō   gozaimasu

なが
長い   →   なご
長う   ございます   is long

oi → ō   tsuyoi   →   tsuyō   gozaimasu

つよ
強い   →   つよ
強う   ございます   is strong

(b) ii → ū   yasashii   →   yasashū*   gozaimasu

やさ
易しい   →   やさ
易しゅう   ございます   is easy

ōkii   →   ōkyū*   gozaimasu

おお
大きい   →   おお
大きゅう   ございます   is big

(c) ui → ū   yasui   →   yasū   gozaimasu

やす
安い   →   やす
安う   ございます   is cheap

* These are the only exceptions: adjectives ending in shii and kii become shū and kyū, respectively, not shiu or kiu.

8

1. あの子はかしこい。 (plain)

こ

That child is bright.

2. コンサートは素晴らしかったです。 (polite)

す ば

The concert was fabulous.

3. 泉先生のご講義はいつも面白うございます。 (honorific)

いずみせんせい   こう ぎ   おもしろ

Professor Izumi's lectures are always interesting.

4. 母の病気は軽うございました。 (humble)

びょう き   かる

My mother's illness was slight.

5. 昨日のピクニックは楽しゅうございました。 (superpolite)

きのう   たの

Yesterday's picnic was fun.

6. お天気がよければ/よかったらホエールウォッチングがございます。 (superpolite)

てん き

If the weather is good, there will be whale watching.

Na-adjectives

When used as predicates, na-adjectives are treated like nouns. The stem (the form without な) is followed by だ, です, or でございます depending on the desired style.

元気な Healthy

	Plain	Polite	Superpolite
Present (is healthy)	元気だ	元気です	(お) 元気でございます
Negative (is not healthy)	元気で (は) ない	元気で (は) ありません	(お) 元気で (は) ございません
Past (was healthy)	元気だった	元気でした	(お) 元気でございました
Negative Past (was not healthy)	元気で (は) なかった	元気で (は) ありませんでした	(お) 元気で (は) ございませんでした
Presumptive (is probably healthy)	元気だろう	元気でしょう	(お) 元気でございましょう
Conditional (if ... is healthy)	元気なら / 元気だったら	元気でしたら	(お) 元気でございましたら

1. 彼女は親切だ。 (plain)

She is kind.

2. 課長はいつも仕事に熱心でした。 (polite)

Our section chief was always enthusiastic about his work.

3. 田中先生はお元気でございます。 (honorific)

Professor Tanaka is well.

4. 手続きは簡単でございました。 (superpolite)

The procedure was simple.

VERBS

The forms of verbs change depending on the speech style being used. The patterns of formation depend not only on the type of verb (regular I, regular II, or irregular) but also on the meaning, since there are a number of special honorific and humble verbs for common words like "go," "come," "be," "see," etc.

Regular I Verbs

The dictionary form is used for the plain style, and the -ます form for the polite style. For the honorific style, the passive form (れる ending) or the pattern お + Vstem + になる is used. For the humble style, お + Vstem + する / いたす is used.

書く Write

	Plain	Polite
Present (write)	書く	書きます
Negative (do not write)	書かない	書きません
Past (wrote)	書いた	書きました
Negative Past (did not write)	書かなかった	書きませんでした
Presumptive (probably write)	書くだろう	書くでしょう
Conditional (if ... write)	書けば 書いたら	—

Note that both the dictionary and -ます forms can be used in the honorific and humble styles of speech depending on the situation or the position of a verb.

10

1. 午後、友達と買い物に行きます。 (polite)

I'm going shopping with my friend this afternoon.

2. 林先生がこの本をお書きになった。 (honorific)

Professor Hayashi wrote this book.

3. 木田部長は火曜日までに帰られるだろう。 (honorific)

General Manager Kida will probably return by Tuesday.

4. 今すぐ行けば、電車に間に合うだろう。 (plain)

If you leave right now, you'll be able to catch the train.

Honorific	Humble
書かれる お書きになる	お書きする お書きいたす
書かれない お書きにならない	お書きしない お書きいたさない
書かれた お書きになった	お書きした お書きいたした
書かれなかった お書きにならなかった	お書きしなかった お書きいたさなかった
書かれるだろう お書きになるだろう	お書きするだろう お書きいたすだろう
書かれれば 書かれたら お書きになれば お書きになったら	お書きすれば お書きしたら お書きいたしたら

5. 私が部長にお話しいたします。　　　　　　　　(humble)

I'll speak to the general manager.

6. 母がお連れするはずです。　　　　　　　　　　(humble)

My mother is supposed to take you there.

7. 今お申し込みになれば、お安うございます。　(honorific)

If you order now, it will be cheaper.

Regular II Verbs

Speech styles for regular II verbs are the same as those for regular I verbs, except that the passive form used for the honorific style has a られる ending instead of a れる one.

答える Answer

	Plain	Polite
Present (answer)	答える	答えます
Negative (do not answer)	答えない	答えません
Past (answered)	答えた	答えました
Negative Past (did not answer)	答えなかった	答えませんでした
Presumptive (probably answer)	答えるだろう	答えるでしょう
Conditional (if ... answer)	答えれば 答えたら	—

Verbs

 11

1. 彼は毎朝6時に起きる。 (plain)
   He gets up at six o'clock every morning.

2. 動物園の前でバスを降りました。 (polite)
   I got off the bus in front of the zoo.

3. 先生はその質問にお答えにならなかった。 (honorific)
   The teacher did not answer that question.

4. その件は、私がお調べいたします。 (humble)
   I will look into the matter.

5. 漢字は木村先生が教えられるだろう。 (honorific)
   Professor Kimura will probably teach kanji.

Honorific	Humble
答えられる / お答えになる	お答えする / お答えいたす
答えられない / お答えにならない	お答えしない / お答えいたさない
答えられた / お答えになった	お答えした / お答えいたした
答えられなかった / お答えにならなかった	お答えしなかった / お答えいたさなかった
答えられるだろう / お答えになるだろう	お答えするだろう / お答えいたすだろう
答えられれば / 答えられたら / お答えになれば / お答えになったら	お答えすれば / お答えしたら / お答えいたしたら

6. ここを8時に出られたら、2時までに向こうにお着きになるでしょう。　　　　　　　　　　　　　　　　　　　　(honorific)

If you leave here at eight o'clock, you'll probably arrive there by two.

Irregular Verbs

The two irregular verbs, 来る (come) and する (do), have special honorific and humble forms as shown in the charts below.

来る Come

	Plain	Polite
Present (come)	来る	来ました
Negative (do not come)	来ない	来ません
Past (came)	来た	来ました
Negative Past (did not come)	来なかった	来ませんでした
Presumptive (probably come)	来るだろう	来るでしょう
Conditional (if … come)	来れば 来たら	—

* special honorific and humble verbs

1. 彼女は地下鉄で会社に来る。 (plain)
   She comes to the office by subway.

2. 小田さんはパーティーに来ませんでした。 (polite)
   Mr. Oda didn't come to the party.

3. お客様はまだおいでになりません。 (honorific)
   The guest has not come yet.

Honorific	Humble
来られる いらっしゃる * おいでになる *	まいる * うかがう *
来られない いらっしゃらない * おいでにならない *	まいらない * うかがわない *
来られた いらっしゃった * おいでになった *	まいった * うかがった *
来られなかった いらっしゃらなかった * おいでにならなかった *	まいらなかった * うかがわなかった *
来られるだろう いらっしゃるだろう * おいでになるだろう *	まいるだろう * うかがうだろう *
来られれば 来られたら いらっしゃれば * いらっしゃったら * おいでになれば * おいでになったら *	まいれば * まいったら * うかがえば * うかがったら *

4. 木田先生がいらっしゃれば泉先生もいらっしゃるでしょう。

(honorific)

If Professor Kida comes, Professor Izumi will probably come too.

5. 父はただ今まいります。 (humble)

My father is coming soon.

6. 明日お宅にうかがうつもりです。 (humble)

I plan to come to your house tomorrow.

する Do

	Plain	Polite
Present (do)	する	します
Negative (do not)	しない	しません
Past (did)	した	しました
Negative Past (did not do)	しなかった	しませんでした
Presumptive (probably do)	するだろう	するでしょう
Conditional (if ... do)	すれば したら	—

* special honorific and humble verbs

1. 今晩、何をしますか。 (polite)
What are you going to do tonight?

2. トムは宿題をしなかった。 (plain)
Tom didn't do his homework.

3. パリで何をなさいましたか。 (honorific)
What did you do in Paris?

4. その説明は次の会議で、課長がされるでしょう。 (honorific)
The section chief will probably explain at the next meeting.

Honorific	Humble
される なさる*	いたす*
されない なさらない*	いたしません*
された なさった*	いたした*
されなかった なさらなかった*	いたさなかった*
されるだろう なさるだろう*	いたすでしょう*
されれば されたら なされば* なさったら*	いたしたら*

5. 電話でご注文なされば、2、3日で届きます。　　　(honorific)

If you order by phone, it will be delivered in a few days.

6. パーティーの準備は私達がいたします。　　　(humble)

We will do the party preparations.

Special Honorific and Humble Verbs

There are special honorific and humble verbs that need not to be in the passive form, nor go through the pattern お + Vstem + になる or お + Vstem + する / いたす, to express respect or humility. The following are some of the most common ones.

Special Honorific and Humble Verbs

	Honorific	Humble
行く (go)	いらっしゃる おいでになる	うかがう * まいる
来る (come)	いらっしゃる おいでになる	うかがう * まいる
いる (be)	いらっしゃる おいでになる	おる
見る (see)	ごらんになる	拝見する
言う (say)	おっしゃる	申す 申し上げる
する (do)	なさる	いたす
思う (think)	—	存じる
聞く (hear)	—	うかがう * うけたまわる

会う (meet)	—	お目にかかる
たずねる (ask)	—	うかがう *
知っている (know)	ご存じだ	存じている
食べる / 飲む (eat/drink)	あがる ** めしあがる **	いただく
やる / あげる (give)	—	さし上げる
もらう (receive)	—	いただく
借りる (borrow)	—	拝借する

* The humble verb うかがう (go, come, hear, ask) may also be used as おうかがいする / おうかがいいたす.

** The honorific verbs あがる / めしあがる may also be used as あがられる / めしあがられる or おあがりになる / おめしあがりになる.

1. 松井先生のご本を拝借いたしました。　　　　　　(humble)

I borrowed Professor Matsui's book.

2. 明日、新社長にお目にかかります。　　　　　　(humble)

We will meet the new president of our company tomorrow.

3. お母様は午後お宅にいらっしゃいますか。　　　　(honorific)

Is your mother at home this afternoon?

はい、おります。　　　　　　　　　　　　(humble)

Yes, she is.

4. ブラウンさんにこの花瓶をさし上げるつもりです。　(humble)
I plan to give this vase to Mrs. Brown.

5. お飲み物は何をめしあがりますか。　(honorific)
What would you like to drink?

6. そのことは課長からうかがった。　(humble)
I heard about it from the section chief.

7. 展覧会はもうごらんになりましたか。　(honorific)
Have you seen the exhibition?

8. 何も申し上げることはございません。　(humble)
I have nothing to say.

9. 秋子さんにこのスカーフをいただいた。　(humble)
I received this scarf from Akiko.

10. 山田さんが結婚なさるのをご存じですか。　(honorific)
Did you know that Miss Yamada is getting married?
はい、存じています。　(humble)
Yes, I know.

MALE AND FEMALE SPEECH

In the polite, honorific, and humble styles, there are few differences between male and female speech. But in the plain style used in casual conversation, there are some obvious ones, especially in the use of sentence-final particles, e.g. ね, よ, わ. Some of these particles are used exclusively by females, others exclusively by males. Sometimes the same particle is used by both genders, but the copula before it is omitted in female speech, as in the first example below. It is worth noting, however, that such distinctions are rapidly disappearing, with young women these days using language that was formerly the domain of men, and vice versa.

15

1. この車はドイツ製だよ。　　　　　　　　　(male/female)

This car was made in Germany, you know.

このジャケットはフランス製よ。　　　　　(female)

This jacket was made in France, you know.

2. 試験は難しかったなあ。　　　　　　　　　(male/female)

The exam was terribly difficult.

オペラは素晴らしかったわあ。　　　　　　(female)

The opera was absolutely fabulous.

3. このレポートは私が書くよ。　　　　　　　(male/female)

I'm going to write this report.

このデータは私が調べるわ / わよ。　　　　(female)

I'm going to check this data.

4. 今日は寒いな。 (male/female)

It's cold today, isn't it?

昨日も寒かったわね。 (female)

It was cold yesterday, too, wasn't it?

5. あんな男と付き合うな。 (male)

Don't associate with that kind of man.

あんな人と話さないの。 (female)

Don't talk with that kind of person.

6. おれはがんばるぞ。 (male)

I'll do my best.

私もがんばるわ / わよ。 (female)

I too will do my best.

7. あとは君に頼んだぜ。 (male)

I'm counting on you to do the rest (of the work).

あとはあなたに頼んだわ / わよ。 (female)

I'm counting on you to do the rest (of the work).

CONVERSATION

In Part I you saw how Japanese words and sentences are formed to fit in different speech styles. Now you are ready to see how they work in real situations. Part II presents various scenes where conversation is carried out at different levels of politeness. Each lesson exposes you to three scenes:

(A) Conversation in the polite style, carried out between/among adults who are not close friends

(B) Casual conversation in the plain style, carried out between/among family members and/or close friends

(C) Conversation in the honorific or humble style, carried out between/among people of different social statuses and/or involving mention of respect-worthy people

In addition to demonstrating speech styles, these scenes introduce you to some of the most common sentence patterns in the Japanese language.

Lesson 1

Introducing People

A Mr. Harada introduces Mr. Smith to Mr. Ono.

スミス　あの人はだれですか。

原田　　小野さんです。ご紹介します。

＊　＊　＊

原田　　小野さん、こちらはアメリカ大使館のスミスさん
　　　　です。

スミス　はじめまして。スミスです。どうぞよろしく。

小野　はじめまして。小野です。どうぞよろしく。

Smith　Who is that over there?

Harada　That's Mr. Ono. I'll introduce you to him.

* * *

Harada　Mr. Ono, this is Mr. Smith from the American Embassy.

Smith　How do you do? I'm Smith. Pleasure to meet you.

Ono　How do you do? I'm Ono. Nice to meet you.

⚠ Notes

1. ご紹介します "I'll introduce you (to him)"
   ご- is an honorific prefix that usually comes before a word of Chinese origin. Often it conveys respect for the other person, but here, because it is attached to 紹介する, a word that describes the speaker's actions, it just conveys politeness.

2. こちら "this (person)"
   こちら is interchangeable with この方 (this person) and is slightly more polite than この人.

Miyoko Nishino introduces her friend Yoshiko Tanaka to her older brother at a party.

17

良子　ちょっと、美代子さん。あの人だれ？

美代子　どの人？

良子　あの背が高くて、ハンサムな男の人。

美代子　<ruby>私<rt>わたし</rt></ruby>の<ruby>兄<rt>あに</rt></ruby>よ。<ruby>紹介<rt>しょうかい</rt></ruby>するわ。

*　*　*

美代子　お<ruby>兄<rt>にい</rt></ruby>さん、こちら<ruby>友達<rt>ともだち</rt></ruby>の<ruby>田中良子<rt>た なか</rt></ruby>さん。

良子　　田中良子です。どうぞよろしく。

兄　　　<ruby>西野<rt>にしの</rt></ruby>です。美代子の兄です。よろしく。

Yoshiko	Look, Miyoko! Who's he?
Miyoko	Who's who?
Yoshiko	That tall, handsome man over there.
Miyoko	Oh, that's my brother. I'll introduce you to him.

* * *

Miyoko	Brother, this is my friend Yoshiko Tanaka.
Yoshiko	I'm Yoshiko Tanaka. Nice to meet you.
Brother	I'm Nishino. Miyoko's brother. Nice to meet you.

! Notes

1. ちょっと "Look!"

ちょっと is an adverb whose basic meaning is "a little" but is also used to get someone's attention, as in "Hey!" "Look!" etc.

2. あの人だれ？ "Who's he?"

This is informal for あの人はだれですか. The particle は and the ending ですか are often dropped in casual conversation.

3. どの人？ "Who's who?"

どの人 is used when you are looking for someone you haven't met before among a group of people.

4. あれ "that (person)"

あれ is used in place of あの人 in very casual conversation to refer to your own family members and other people of your in-group.

5. よ / わ (sentence-final particles)

The particle よ at the end of a sentence is used to emphasize the statement, and わ to soften it. よ is used by both male and female speakers, while わ is used mainly by female speakers. But the way Miyoko uses よ in this sentence—兄よ—is feminine; a male speaker would say 兄だよ.

C **A receptionist introduces Ms. Yano to Professor Yoshioka at a professional gathering.**

受付   どちら様でいらっしゃいますか。

矢野   毎朝新聞の矢野です。東大学の吉岡先生はどの方

　　　でしょうか。

受付   あの茶色の背広の方でございます。ご紹介いたし

　　　ます。

* * *

受付   吉岡先生、こちらは毎朝新聞の矢野さんでいらっ

　　　しゃいます。

矢野　はじめまして。矢野でございます。<u>どうぞよろし</u>

　　　<u>くお願^{ねが}いいたします。</u>

吉岡　はじめまして。吉岡です。どうぞよろしく。

Receptionist　May I ask who you might be?

Yano　　　　　I'm Yano from the *Maicho Newspaper*. Which one is Professor Yoshioka of Higashi University?

Receptionist　That person in the brown suit. I'll introduce you to him.

* * *

Receptionist　Professor Yoshioka, this is Ms. Yano from the *Maicho Newspaper*.

Yano　　　　　How do you do? I'm Yano. It's a pleasure to meet you.

Yoshioka　　　How do you do? I'm Yoshioka. Nice to meet you.

⚠ Notes

1. どちら様でいらっしゃいますか "**May I ask who you might be?**"

   どちら様 is the superpolite form for "who," and でいらっしゃいますか is the honorific form of ですか.

2. どの方 "**which person**"

   This is a politer form of どの人^{ひと} (who).

3. でございます "**is**"

   This is the superpolite form of です.

4. ご紹介いたします "**I'll introduce you (to him)**"

   This is a humble form of 紹介します. ご- is a polite prefix, and

いたす is the humble form of する. The pattern ご- / お- + N + する / いたす can be used for any number of する-verbs whose noun base is a kanji compound. In most cases, ご- is the appropriate prefix, but sometimes お- is used.

5. どうぞよろしくお願いいたします **"It's a pleasure to meet you"**
The phrase お願いいたします (lit. I beg you) is used when making a humble request. どうぞよろしくお願いいたします means "I beg you to favor me." This combination is far more polite than どうぞよろしく and is used in very formal speech.

 Practice

Circle the correct word from among the options in parentheses.

1. 先生、こちらは私の (お父さん / 父) です。
Professor, this is my father.

2. あの方は (だれ / どなた / どの方) ですか。
Who is that person over there?

3. 人事課の木田さんはどの人 (です / でいらっしゃいます / でございます) か。
Which one is Mr. Kida of the personnel section?

4. 課長、こちらは私の母 (でいらっしゃいます / でございます / です)。
Chief, this is my mother.

5. 私がマネージャーの宮田 (でいらっしゃいます / でございます / です)。(どちら様 / だれ / どの方) でいらっしゃいますか。
I'm Miyata, the manager. May I ask who you are?

Lesson 2

Identifying Things

A A passenger asks a cab driver about an interesting building he sees from the window.

19

乗客　あれは何ですか。

運転手　あのガラスの建物ですか。新しい美術館です。

乗客　珍しい建築ですねえ。何の美術館ですか。

運転手　近代芸術の美術館です。

Passenger　What is that?

Driver　That glass building? That's a new art museum.

Passenger What unusual architecture! What kind of museum is it?

Driver It's a museum for modern arts.

Note

1. ねえ (sentence-final particle)

The particle ねえ at the end of a sentence indicates emotion or admiration. It is used by both male and female speakers.

B A daughter returns home, finds her mother looking at something, and asks what it is.

20

娘 ただいま。お母さん、それ何?

母 宝石箱よ。

娘 だれの?　お母さんの?

母 あなたのおばあさんのよ。

娘 指輪にネックレスにイヤリング。すごいわねえ。

Daughter I'm home! What is that, Mother?

Mother It's a jewelry box.

Daughter Whose? Yours?

Mother Your grandmother's.

Daughter Rings, necklaces, earrings … how marvelous!

! Notes

1. それ何？ "What's that?"

This is the casual equivalent of それは何ですか and is used by male and female speakers alike. The particle は and the ending ですか are dropped in informal speech. The more blunt それ何 だ is used only by male speakers.

2. だれの？　お母さんの？ "Whose? Yours, Mother?"

More omissions. In both sentences, ですか is left out.

3. のよ (sentence-final particles)

のよ is an emphatic particle combination used by female speakers.

4. 指輪にネックレスに… "rings, necklaces, and …"

The pattern N + に + N + に indicates a number of things added one after another. The idea is earrings in addition to rings, necklaces, and other fine pieces of jewelry.

5. わねえ (sentence-final particles)

The particle combination わねえ (where ね is elongated) at the end of a sentence expresses emotion or admiration, and is used by female speakers.

After letting a group of tourists off a bus, the guide finds an umbrella left behind and looks for its owner.

ガイド 皆様、こちらがバス・ターミナルでございます。

本日は、まことにありがとうございました。

* * *

ガイド これはどなたの傘でしょうか。お客様 のでは？

客 いいえ、私のじゃございません。あの学生さんの

じゃないですか。

学生 あっ、それ僕のです。すみません。

Guide Ladies and gentlemen, this is the bus terminal. Thank you very much (for taking the tour with us) today.

* * *

Guide Whose umbrella might this be? Yours, ma'am?

Tourist No, it's not mine. Doesn't it belong to that student over there?

Student Oh, that's mine. Thanks.

⚠ Notes

1. 本日 "today"
   本日 is more formal than 今日.

2. まことにありがとうございました "thank you very much"
   まことに is more formal than 本当に. The guide uses the past tense ありがとうございました rather than the present to thank the tourists for their patronage. This is because their patronage has come to an end—the trip is over.

3. どなたの "whose"
   どなたの is more polite than だれの.

4. お客様 "customer," "client," "guest"
   お客様 is used by salespersons and hotel or airline employees to address customers.

5. のでは？ "Is it ...?"
   The superpolite ending ございませんか is omitted from the sentence because the meaning is clear without it.

6. じゃございません "is not"
   じゃ is a contraction of では. 傘 (umbrella) is omitted after 私の because it is obvious what is being talked about. The speaker uses the polite form ございません instead of ありません (even though she is speaking to a tour guide) because she is somewhat elderly, and elderly people tend to use polite language. No respect or humility is implied by ございません here.

7. すみません "thanks"
   すみません is used to express gratitude or apology. The meaning depends on the circumstances. Here it means "thank you."

Practice

Place an O next to the sentence if the usage of words is appropriate and an X if it is not.

1. 先生、これはあなたの辞書ですか。

   Professor, is this your dictionary?

2. 林さん、あの大きな箱は何ですか。

   Ms. Hayashi, what is that big box over there?

3. 田村君、これ、お前の車？　すごいわねえ。

   Tamura, is this your car? Fabulous!

4. お客様、これ、だれのカメラですか。

   Sir, whose camera is this?

5. 「杉本課長、これは何のレポートでしょうか」
   「あの企画のガイドラインだろう」

   "Chief Sugimoto, what is this report about?"
   "It's probably the guidelines for the proposal."

Lesson ③

Asking When

A　Two middle-aged women who are on a group tour and happen to share a hotel room talk about the itinerary for the day.

22

田村　今、何時ですか。

今井　まだ6時前です。

田村　ここの朝食は7時からですね？

今井　ええ、そうです。バスは9時に出発します。

田村　今日の観光は4時半までですね？

今井　ええ。

Tamura	What time is it now?
Imai	It's not even six o'clock yet.
Tamura	Breakfast here begins at seven o'clock, right?
Imai	That's right. Our bus leaves at nine.
Tamura	Today's sightseeing ends at four thirty, doesn't it?
Imai	That's right.

🛈 Note

1. ね **"right?" "isn't it?" "don't you think?"**

The particle ね at the end of a sentence is used to solicit confirmation or agreement from one's listener. It is used by both male and female speakers.

B Two sisters talk about the date and time of their friend's wedding ceremony.

23

妹 お姉さん、野田さんの結婚式は何曜日？

姉 来週の土曜日。6月5日よ。

妹 式は何時に始まるの？

姉 1時半からよ。

妹 ここから教会まで、どのぐらいかかるかしら？

姉 電車で20分ぐらいでしょうね。

Younger Sister	Sister, what day (of the week) is Miss Noda's wedding ceremony?
Older Sister	Next Saturday. June fifth.
Younger Sister	What time does the ceremony start?
Older Sister	One thirty.
Younger Sister	I wonder how long it takes from here to the church.
Older Sister	Probably about twenty minutes by train.

⚠ Notes

1. 始まるの？ "start?"

始まるの？ is the plain-style equivalent of 始まるのですか; where the particle の is spoken with a rising intonation. の as a question marker is used mainly by female speakers. Male speakers use either no particle (いつ始まる?) or んだ (いつ始まるんだ?).

2. かしら？ "I wonder ..."

The particle かしら at the end of a sentence poses an indirect question or doubt, and is used only by female speakers.

3. でしょう (**presumptive form of** です)

Note that although this conversation is casual and carried out between family members, the speakers sometimes use polite language such as でしょう. This is a characteristic of female speech—women tend to talk more politely. If it were two brothers speaking, the older would have probably used だろう, which is the plain-style form.

学生　八木先生、いらっしゃいますか。

助手　いいえ、あいにく今ご旅行中ですが……。先日イ

タリアへ行かれました。

学生　そうですか。いつお帰りになりますか。

助手　今月末までに帰られます。

学生　学校には、いつご出勤になりますか。

助手　来月6日に出勤されます。

学生　では、その頃またうかがいます。

Student	Is Professor Yagi in?
Assistant	No, I'm sorry to say (lit. unfortunately) he is away on (lit. in the midst of) a trip right now. He went to Italy the other day.
Student	Is that so? When will he come back?
Assistant	He'll come back by the end of this month.
Student	When will he be back to school (lit. come to work)?
Assistant	He'll be back on the sixth of next month.
Student	Well then, I'll come again around that time.

⚠ Notes

1. いらっしゃいますか "Is he in?"
   いらっしゃいます is the polite form of the special honorific verb
   いらっしゃる, meaning "to be."

2. ご旅行中ですが…… "is in the midst of a trip …"
   The particle が at the end of a sentence serves to soften the
   tone of the sentence. あいにく今ご旅行中ですが is less direct
   than あいにく今ご旅行中です.

3. 行かれました "went"
   行かれました is the passive, past-tense, polite form of 行く and
   is used for the honorific style.

4. お帰りになります "will come back"
   The pattern お + Vstem + になる is honorific. This is one of two
   forms an honorific verb can take, the other being the passive
   form. See the next note.

5. 帰られます "will come back"
   This is the passive, polite form of 帰る and is used for the honorific style. This is slightly less polite than お帰りになります.

6. ご出勤になります "will come to work"
   This is an honorific verb form. In the case of a する-verb like 出
   勤する, where する attaches to a kanji compound, the honorific
   form is ご + N + になる. This is the same level of honorific as
   お + Vstem + になる (Note 4 above).

7. 出勤されます "will come to work"
   出勤されます is the passive, polite form of 出勤する and is honorific. This is slightly less polite than ご出勤になります.

8. うかがいます "will come"

うかがいます is the polite form of the special humble verb うかがう, meaning "to come" or "to go." It can also mean "to hear" or "to ask."

 Practice

Rewrite the following sentences using the words given. Hint: Use honorific or polite forms.

1. 主人は毎朝8時に出勤します。

→ 隣のご主人は＿＿＿＿＿＿＿＿＿＿＿＿＿＿＿＿。

My husband goes to work at eight o'clock every morning.

→ My neighbor's husband …

2. お姉さん、何時に出かけるの？

→ 社長、＿＿＿＿＿＿＿＿＿＿＿＿＿＿＿＿。

Sister, what time should we leave?

→ Mr. President, …?

3. 木田さん、今日のミーティングは何時から？

→ 課長、＿＿＿＿＿＿＿＿＿＿＿＿＿＿＿＿。

Ms. Kida, what time is today's meeting?

→ Chief, …?

4. 弟は先週ヨーロッパから帰りました。

→ 原先生は＿＿＿＿＿＿＿＿＿＿＿＿＿＿＿。

My younger brother returned from Europe last week.

→ Professor Hara …

5. 私が水曜日までにうかがいます。

→ 小川さんの息子さんが＿＿＿＿＿＿＿＿＿＿＿＿＿＿＿＿＿。

I will come by Wednesday.

→ Mr. Ogawa's son …

Lesson 4

Asking Where

A On an unfamiliar street, a man asks a passerby how he can get to where he is heading.

25

男の人 すみません。郵便局はどこにありますか。

通行人 あそこに白いビルがありますね。あのビルの隣です。

男の人 ああ、そうですか。それから、この近くにいいレ

ストランはありますか。

通行人 ええ、郵便局の後ろにありますよ。

男の人　どうもありがとう。

通行人　いいえ。

Man　　　Excuse me, where is the post office?

Passerby　Do you see the white building over there? It's next to that building.

Man　　　Oh, I see. And is there a good restaurant near here?

Passerby　Yes, there is one behind the post office.

Man　　　Thank you.

Passerby　Not at all.

！ Notes

1. すみません "excuse me"

   すみません, which means "thank you" or "sorry" in other situations, is used here to get someone's attention.

2. にあります → です "It is …"

   あります may be replaced by です when the meaning is clear from the context: ビルの隣にあります → ビルの隣です. Note that the particle に is not used before です.

3. 近くに "near"

   近く is a noun form of the i-adjective 近い (near) and is used to mean "vicinity." It takes the particle に when one is talking about the location of something nearby.

A young couple—tourists on their first visit to Tokyo—get lost and try to figure out where they are.

妻（つま）　ここはどこ？

夫（おっと）　さあ、どこかな？

妻　一番近（いちばんちか）い地下鉄（ちかてつ）の駅（えき）はこの地図（ちず）でどこ？

夫　あっ、ここだ。ここから二（ふた）つ目（め）の角（かど）だ。

妻　あそこにお巡（まわ）りさんがいるわ。聞（き）いたら？

夫　いいよ。さあ、行（い）こう。

Wife	Where are we?
Husband	Jeez, I wonder….
Wife	Where is the nearest subway station on this map?
Husband	Oh, here it is. At the corner two blocks from here.
Wife	There's a policeman over there. How about asking him?
Husband	Forget it. Let's go.

Notes

1. どこかな？ "**I wonder where we are.**"

The particle かな at the end of a sentence poses an indirect question or doubt—just like かしら from Lesson 3 (Note 2, p. 52).

2. 一番近い "**the nearest**"

This is the superlative form of the adjective 近い.

3. 聞いたら？ **"How about asking (him)?"**

The -たら form (Vtara) is used for making a suggestion in casual conversation. In more polite speech, it might be followed by どうですか or どうでしょうか.

4. いいよ **"Forget it"**

This いいよ does not mean "okay," it means the opposite. いい is sometimes used (with or without よ or another emphatic particle or particle combination) to reject a suggestion. The usage comes from いい's meaning "good," "adequate," "sufficient."

5. 行こう **"Let's go"**

行こう is the volitional form of 行く and expresses a suggestion.

C In the quiet suburbs of Tokyo, an elderly woman stops a student hurriedly passing by and asks her where she can find the house she is looking for.

27

女の人　あのう、ちょっとおうかがいいたしますが……。

清水さんのお宅はどちらでしょうか。

学生　ええと、清水さんですか。お医者さんの清水さん

ですね？

女の人　いいえ、建築家の清水先生なんですが。

学生　建築家の清水さん？　ああ、清水道夫さんです

ね？

59

女の人　はい、そうです。このお近くですか。

学生　ええ、あの青い屋根の家です。

女の人　そうですか。どうもありがとうございました。

学生　どういたしまして。

Woman Uh, excuse me, may I ask … which house is Mr. Shimizu's?

Student Let me see … Mr. Shimizu? That's Mr. Shimizu the doctor, isn't it?

Woman No, Mr. Shimizu the architect.

Student Mr. Shimizu the architect? Oh, you mean Michio Shimizu?

Woman That's right. Is it near here?

Student Yes, it's that house with the blue roof.

Woman Is that so? Thank you very much.

Student You're welcome.

! Notes

1. あのう "Uh, excuse me"
   あのう (pronounced hesitantly) is used in place of, or together with, すみません to get someone's attention.

2. おうかがいいたしますが "May I ask …?"
   おうかがいいたしますが is a superpolite way to begin a question. It consists of the special humble verb うかがう (ask) in the お + Vstem + いたす pattern, where いたす is the humble form of する. The particle が at the end is acting as a softener, making the sentence sound less direct.

3. どちら "which," "where"

The woman could have used どこ, as in 清水さんのお宅はどこで しょうか (Where is Mr. Shimizu's house?), but どちら is more polite.

4. 清水先生なんです "It's Mr. Shimizu"

先生 is used not only for teachers but also for others who hold respected professions. なん, the colloquial form of なの, emphasizes the noun that precedes it. なんです is used after nouns and the stems of na-adjectives when trying to explain something; after i-adjectives and verbs, のです is used (without the な).

5. お近く "near"

The honorific prefix お- is attached to 近く, a noun form of the adjective 近い, to make the word sound elegant.

 Practice

What would you say in the following situations?

1. You want to ask a police officer where the nearest bus stop (バス停) is.

2. You want to ask a passerby where you are.

3. You want to ask your mother where your younger brother Takashi is.

4. You want to ask your teacher where Professor Sasaki is.

5. You want to ask a stranger whether there is a bakery (パン屋) nearby.

Describing States

A Mr. Seki asks Mr. Hara, who has just joined the company, about his new apartment.

関 今度のアパートはどうですか。

原 いいですよ。明るくて、かなり広いです。

関 駅に近いですか。

原 はい、歩いて5、6分です。スーパーにも近いし、とても便利です。

関 家賃が高いでしょう？

原　　いいえ、そんなに高くないですよ。

関　　それはよかったですね。

Seki	How is your new apartment?
Hara	Good. It's bright and fairly large.
Seki	Is it near the station?
Hara	Yes, it's a five- or six-minute walk. It's also close to the supermarket, and it's very convenient.
Seki	The rent is high, isn't it?
Hara	No, it's not that high.
Seki	That's great!

⚠ Notes

1. 歩いて "on foot"

   歩いて is the -て form of 歩く (walk) and expresses how an action is performed (i.e. "on foot").

2. 近いし "is close, and moreover …"

   The particle し attached to an adjective in the plain form is used as a conjunction to link two or more states, with the nuance that the first state does not give a complete picture of the situation.

3. 高いでしょう？ "is high, isn't it?"

   でしょう is the polite, presumptive form of です, here attached to the i-adjective 高い (expensive). でしょう (or its plain-style equivalent だろう) can be used with a rising or falling intonation to confirm something. In this usage, it is similar to the particle ね (isn't it? right?) at the end of a sentence (Note 1, p. 51).

Masao asks his girlfriend, Hisako, about her new boss.

正夫　新しいボスはどう？

久子　悪くないわ。彼は性格があっさりしているし、仕事にも熱心よ。

正夫　きつくない？

久子　ううん、そんなことないわよ。割に親切よ。

正夫　そう。よかったね。

Masao　How is your new boss?
Hisako　Not bad. He's openhearted, and he's enthusiastic about work, too.
Masao　He's not strict?
Hisako　No, not at all. He's rather kind.
Masao　I see. That's great!

! Notes

1. **どう？ "How is …?"**
   どう？ is a shortening of どうですか and can be used by both male and female speakers. A more masculine way of saying it would be どうだ？

2. 彼は性格があっさりしている "He's openhearted"

The literal meaning of 彼は性格があっさりしている is "As for him, his personality is light." It helps to think of 性格があっさりしている as a set phrase meaning "openhearted."

3. 熱心よ (feminine speech)

See Note 6 below.

4. きつくない？ "He's not strict?"

This is another question, in the plain style, that can be used by both male and female speakers. A more masculine way of saying it would be きつくないか.

5. ううん "no"

ううん for "no" and うん for "yes" are used by both male and female speakers only in casual conversation.

6. わよ。割に親切よ (feminine speech)

わよ is overtly feminine, as is よ following a noun or the stem of a na-adjective. 割に is an adverb meaning "relatively," "comparatively," etc.

C A secretary starts a conversation with her boss, the president of the company, who has just returned from a trip.

30

秘書　お帰りなさいませ。ご旅行はいかがでしたか。

社長　よかったよ。天気はいいし、ゴルフには最高だったな。

秘書 　それはよろしゅうございましたね。ところで、あのホテルはお気にめされましたか。

社長 　ああ、静かだったし、食事はうまかったし、申し分なかったよ。この次もあそこがいいね。

秘書 　はい、わかりました。

Secretary   Welcome back. How was your trip?

President   It was good. The weather was fine—perfect for golfing.

Secretary   I'm glad to hear that. By the way, did you like the hotel (I reserved for you)?

President   Yes, it was quiet, the food was good … it was ideal (lit. it had no flaws). I'd like to stay there next time, too.

Secretary   You got it.

! Notes

1. お帰りなさいませ "Welcome back"

   お帰り, or the politer お帰りなさい, is a set expression used to welcome someone back home or to an office. ませ, the imperative form of ます (an auxiliary verb that expresses respect for the listener), is added for extra politeness.

2. いかが "how"

   いかが is a politer word for どう.

3. な (sentence-final particle)

   The particle な at the end of a sentence expresses emotion and is used by both male and female speakers.

4. よろしゅうございました "good"

よろしゅうございました is a superpolite expression. The i-adjective よろしい (a politer form of いい) changes to よろしゅう before ございます / ございました.

5. お気にめされましたか "Did you like it?"

お気にめす is a special honorific verb meaning "like" whose non-honorific equivalents are 気に入る and 好む. Here it is used in the passive, and in the past tense.

6. うまかった "was delicious/good"

The informal i-adjective うまい (delicious) is used mostly by male speakers, while the more standard おいしい is used by both male and female speakers.

 Practice

Translate the following sentences using appropriate levels of politeness.

1. Akira speaking to his friend Tom:

   "Tom, how was yesterday's exam (試験)?"
   "It wasn't too hard (難しい)."

2. Mrs. Oda speaking to her neighbor, Mrs. Kubo:

   "The vegetables (野菜) at that supermarket are fresh (新鮮な) and cheap (安い), aren't they?"
   "Yes, they are."

3. Nobuko speaking to her friend Yasuko:

"My new piano teacher has a gentle (優^やしい) nature, and what's
more, she is kind (親切^{しんせつ}な)."

"That's great!"

4. A secretary speaking to her boss in the superpolite style:

"Mr. President, was your trip enjoyable (楽^{たの}しい)?"

"It was perfect (flawless)."

5. A mother speaking to her son Kazuo, who has just come back
from school:

"Welcome home, Kazuo. How was today's lunch (お弁当^{べんとう})? Good?"

"Yeah, it was."

Making Comparisons

 A Mr. Ueda steps into a watchmaker's and looks for a graduation gift for his son.

 31

店員<ruby>店員<rt>てんいん</rt></ruby>　いらっしゃいませ。

上田<ruby>上田<rt>うえだ</rt></ruby>　その時計<ruby>時計<rt>とけい</rt></ruby>はスイス製<ruby>製<rt>せい</rt></ruby>ですか。

店員　はい、とても<u>正確<ruby>正確<rt>せいかく</rt></ruby>で評判<ruby>評判<rt>ひょうばん</rt></ruby>がいい</u>商品<ruby>商品<rt>しょうひん</rt></ruby>です。

上田　それ、いくらですか。

店員　3万円<ruby>万円<rt>まんえん</rt></ruby>です。

上田　ちょっと高<ruby>高<rt>たか</rt></ruby>いですね。もう少<ruby>少<rt>すこ</rt></ruby>し<u>安<ruby>安<rt>やす</rt></ruby>い</u>のはありませ

んか。これは？

店員 こちらは日本製(にほんせい)でそちらより少し安いです。
2万3千円(ぜんえん)です。こちらもそちらと同(おな)じくらい正
確です。

上田 じゃあ、これをください。

店員 はい、ありがとうございます。

Clerk   Welcome (to our store).

Ueda   Is that watch a Swiss make?

Clerk   Yes, it's a very accurate and popular product.

Ueda   How much is it?

Clerk   It's 30,000 yen.

Ueda   That's a little expensive. Do you have a less-expensive one?
How about this one?

Clerk   This one is a Japan-make and is a little cheaper than that one.
It's 23,000 yen. This one is about as accurate as that one.

Ueda   Well, I'll take this one (lit. Give me this one, please).

Clerk   You got it. Thank you very much.

! Notes

1. いらっしゃいませ "Welcome"
   いらっしゃい, or the politer いらっしゃいませ, is used to welcome
   a customer to a store or a guest to one's home.

2. 正確で評判がいい "**accurate and popular**"

A more literal translation of 評判がいい would be "has a good reputation." The watch is accurate and has a good reputation—hence it is popular.

3. 安いの "**an inexpensive one**"

The particle の after the i-adjective 安い creates a pronoun, in this case meaning "a less-expensive one."

4. そちらより安い "**a little cheaper than that one**"

The pattern N + より indicates an item the subject is being compared to in some way (i.e. the subject has more or less of some quality than N).

5. そちらと同じくらい正確です "**is about as accurate as that one**"

The pattern N1 + は + N2 + と同じくらい / ぐらい + Adj is used when the compared items are just about the same. In this case, the pronouns こちら and そちら stand in for N1 and N2, and は is replaced by も.

B Tomiko and Haruko—two women—talk about taking their friend Hiroko out to lunch for her birthday.

32

登美子　弘子のお誕生日のランチ、どこがいい？

春子　中国料理とイタリア料理と、どっちがいいかな？

登美子　彼女、イタリア料理のほうが好きよ。

春子 　それじゃ、郵便局の前の新しいレストランはどう？

　　　あそこ、とても評判がいいのよ。

登美子 　そうなの？　あたしはどこでもいいわ。

春子 　何時にしようか？　11時と、12時と、1時の中で、

　　　いつが一番都合がいい？

登美子 　私は12時が一番いいわ。でも、まず彼女に聞か

　　　なきゃ。

春子 　そうね。

Tomiko　Where would be a good place for Hiroko's birthday lunch?

Haruko　I wonder which would be better—Chinese or Italian….

Tomiko　She likes Italian better.

Haruko　Then how about the new restaurant in front of the post office? It's very popular.

Tomiko　Really? Any place will be fine with me.

Haruko　What time shall we make it? When is the most convenient for you—eleven o'clock, twelve o'clock, or one o'clock?

Tomiko　Twelve o'clock is best for me. But we should ask Hiroko first.

Haruko　You're right.

⚠ **Notes**

1. 中国料理とイタリア料理と、どっちが…… **"Between Chinese and Italian, which is …?"**
The pattern N1 + と + N2 + と、どっちが is used to make a comparative question. どっち is the colloquial form of どちら.

2. イタリア料理のほう **lit. "the side of Italian food"**
The pattern N + のほう indicates a choice between two items in question. ほう is a noun that literally means "side" or "direction."

3. 好きよ **"likes …"**
よ by itself is an emphatic sentence-final particle used by both male and female speakers, but this particular combination of a na-adjective stem followed by よ is overtly feminine. The masculine to gender-neutral pattern would be 好きだよ.

4. それじゃ **"then," "well," "in that case"**
それじゃ is a contraction of それでは.

5. のよ (sentence-final particles)
The particle combination のよ is used by female speakers and functions to emphasize the statement that comes before it.

6. そうなの？ **"Really?"**
This is also used mainly by female speakers. The masculine equivalent would be そうか？ with a rising intonation.

7. あたし **"I"**
In informal conversation, female speakers sometimes use あたし instead of 私.

8. 何時にしようか？ **"What time shall we make it?"**

The pattern N + にする means "make it N" and is used in stating decisions. Here する is in the polite volitional form, followed by the question-forming particle か:

9. 11時と、12時と、1時の中で、いつが一番…… "**When is the most … among eleven o'clock, twelve o'clock, and one o'clock?**"
The pattern N1 + と + N2 + と + N3 + の中で、いつが一番 is used to make a comparative question that involves three choices.

10. 聞かなきゃ "**must ask**"
聞かなきゃ（ならない）is a contraction of 聞かなければ（ならない）, meaning "must ask" or "have to ask."

11. そうね "**You're right,**" "**I agree**"
Again, this is feminine. A more masculine form (also used by women) would be そうだね. And the polite, gender-neutral form would be そうですね.

C A middle-aged couple consult with a travel agent about their plans for a vacation to Hokkaido.

33

エージェント　北海道<ruby>北海道<rt>ほっかいどう</rt></ruby>ツアーにはこの<ruby>三<rt>みっ</rt></ruby>つのプランがござい

ますが。どうぞこれをごらんになってください。

<ruby>夫<rt>おっと</rt></ruby>　　　ＡプランのほうがＢプランよりツアー<ruby>費<rt>ひ</rt></ruby>が<ruby>安<rt>やす</rt></ruby>

いですね。

エージェント　はい、Ｂプランはホテルが<ruby>少<rt>すこ</rt></ruby>し<ruby>お高<rt>たか</rt></ruby>くなって

おります。

妻　　　　　Cプランが<ruby>一番<rt>いちばん</rt></ruby>安いんですね。

エージェント　はい、あちらでのバスツアーが<u>ほかのプラン</u>
<u>ほど</u>多くございません。その<ruby>代<rt>か</rt></ruby>わりフリータイ
ムがもっとございます。

妻　　　　　あなた、フリータイムが多いほうがいいんじゃ
ない？

夫　　　　　そうだな。

エージェント　Cプランがよろしゅうございますか。この三つ
の<ruby>中<rt>なか</rt></ruby>で、これが一番お<ruby>客様<rt>きゃくさま</rt></ruby>に<ruby>人気<rt>にんき</rt></ruby>がございます。

夫　　　　　じゃあ、それでお<ruby>願<rt>ねが</rt></ruby>いします。

エージェント　かしこまりました。

Agent　　For Hokkaido tours, we offer these three plans. Please take a look at these. (hands the couple some pamphlets)

Husband　The tour expenses of Plan A are cheaper than those of Plan B, aren't they?

Agent　　Yes, in Plan B the hotel is a little more expensive.

Wife　　Plan C is the cheapest, isn't it?

Agent　　Yes. It doesn't have as many bus tours as the other plans have. Instead, it includes more free time.

Wife   Isn't it better to have more free time, dear?

Husband   I think so.

Agent   Would you like Plan C? Among the three, it's the most popular with our customers.

Husband   Well, we'll take it, then.

Agent   Certainly, sir.

⚠ Notes

1. ごらんになってください "**Please take a look**"
ごらんになる is a special honorific verb meaning "see," "look," or "watch."

2. おります "**is/are**"
おる / おります is a special humble verb used in place of いる / います.

3. んです "**is/are**"
The particle の followed by です usually becomes んです in conversation. んです is used when the speaker is explaining something or asking for an explanation or a reason. This is the same as なんです (Note 4, p. 61), except that what comes before it must be an i-adjective or a verb in the plain form.

4. ほかのプランほど…ございません "**has not as … as the other plans**"
The pattern N + ほど…ない indicates that one item (the subject) does not have the attribute that another item (N) has, or at least not to the same extent.

5. いいんじゃない？ "**Isn't it good?**"
いいんじゃない？ is informal for いいのではありませんか.

6. かしこまりました "Certainly"

かしこまりました is used toward superiors or customers as a humble expression of assent to orders or requests.

 Practice

What would be the appropriate thing to ask or say in the following situations?

1. Tom asks the store clerk how much that jacket (ジャケット) costs.

2. Masako asks her friend Linda what she likes better, sushi or tempura.

3. Jim tells his teacher that today's test (テスト) was easier (易しい) than yesterday's.

4. Mr. Toda wonders who is the most competent (有能な) among the three newcomers (新入社員).

5. Ms. Hayashi, who has just returned from Kyushu, tells Mrs. Imai, her superior's wife, that it was just about as hot (暑い) as Tokyo but wasn't as humid (蒸し暑い).

Lesson 7

Describing Actions in the Present, Future, and Past

 A Mrs. Aoki sees Linda, a student who has recently moved into the neighborhood, waiting at a bus stop and goes over to chat with her.

青木　こんにちは、リンダさん。どちらへ？　お買い物ですか。

リンダ　ええ、スーパーで買い物をして、それから友達の家へ行きます。そこで今晩パーティーがあるんですよ。

青木　そうですか。お友達はアメリカの方ですか。

リンダ　ええ、でも日本の友達も来ます。みんなで一緒に

　　　　おすしを作ったり、てんぷらを揚げたりします。

青木　　それは、いいわね！　リンダさんはお料理が好き

　　　　なんですね。

リンダ　ええ、下手ですが……。

青木　　あっ、バスが来ました。じゃあ、<u>お気をつけて</u>。

Aoki   Hello, Linda. Where to? Going shopping?

Linda   Yes, I'm going to do some shopping at the supermarket, and
        after that I'm going to my friend's house. We're having a
        party there tonight.

Aoki   Is that so? Is your friend American?

Linda   Yes, but some Japanese friends are coming too. Together
        we're going to make sushi and fry tempura, and do other
        things like that.

Aoki   How nice! You like cooking, don't you?

Linda   Yes, though I'm not good at it....

Aoki   Oh, the bus has come. Well, take care.

⚠ Notes

1. パーティーがあるんです "We are having a party"
   Linda uses あるんです instead of あります because she is explaining the circumstances to Mrs. Aoki.

2. お気をつけて "Take care"
   お気をつけて, or the slightly less polite 気をつけて, is used to

bid farewell to someone going off on a trip and means "Have a good trip."

B **Akira asks Sam how he spent his weekend.**

明 サム、週末はどうだった？

サム よかったよ。友達と一緒に箱根へ行って、湖で
モーターボートに乗ったり魚を釣ったりしたよ。

明 箱根で泊った？

サム うん、湖のそばの旅館に泊ったよ。部屋から富士
山がよく見えたよ。

明 マイクも一緒？

サム いや、彼は彼女とデートだったんだ。

明 そうか。ところで、今晩ビヤホールで飲む？

サム だめだよ。明日は試験だから。

Akira　How was your weekend, Sam?
Sam　It was wonderful. I went to Hakone with some friends. We rode a motorboat on the lake and caught fish.

Akira	Did you stay overnight in Hakone?
Sam	Yeah, we stayed at a Japanese-style inn near the lake. From the room we could see Mt. Fuji clearly (lit. Mt. Fuji was clearly visible).
Akira	Was Mike with you?
Sam	No, he had a date with his girlfriend.
Akira	Oh. By the way, want to go for drinks this evening at the beer hall?
Sam	I can't. I've got an exam tomorrow.

! Notes

1. サム "Sam"

   In the previous dialogue, Mrs. Aoki addressed Linda as リンダ さん. Here Akira addresses Sam as サム, without さん or any other courtesy title. Sometimes Japanese people use さん after the first name of a foreigner—in keeping with the practice of applying it to Japanese names—and sometimes not, because the tradition doesn't exist in other languages and some feel it is friendlier to adapt to the foreigner's culture. Either form is acceptable, and a foreign given name without さん is not rude. Here, of course, Akira and Sam are good friends, so さん or 君 would almost be awkward.

2. どうだった？ "How was it?"

   どうだった？ is the casual equivalent of どうでしたか, and may be used by both male and female speakers. どうだ？ (present tense) is used only by male speakers.

3. 富士山がよく見えた "we could see Mt. Fuji clearly," "Mt. Fuji was clearly visible"

   見える is a special verb of sensation that describes something

4. いや "no"

   いや is used by male speakers.

5. だめだよ "I can't"

   だめ is a na-adjective meaning "no good" or "not allowed." だめだよ, a casual equivalent of だめですよ, is used only by male speakers. Female speakers use だめよ.

C Mrs. Tokuda speaks to Mr. Young, her son's teacher, who has recently come to Japan to teach English.

36

徳田　先生はもう日本の生活にお慣れになりましたか。

ヤング　はい、おかげ様で大分落ち着きました。

徳田　日本の食べ物をめしあがりますか。

ヤング　もちろん、大好きです。前の家がサンフランシスコで、友達とよく日本食のレストランへ行って、さしみやすき焼きやてんぷらなどを食べました。

徳田　まあ、そうなんですか。じゃあ、日本酒もめしあがりますね。

ヤング　ええ、時々。ウイスキーのほうが好きですけど。

徳田　お料理はご自分でなさいます？

ヤング　自分で作ったり外で食べたりです。

Tokuda Mr. Young, have you gotten used to Japanese life?

Young Yes, thankfully I've more or less settled down.

Tokuda Do you eat Japanese food?

Young Of course, I love it. My former house was in San Francisco, and I often went to Japanese restaurants with my friends and had sashimi, sukiyaki, tempura, and other dishes.

Tokuda Is that so? Then you drink sake, too, don't you?

Young Yes, sometimes. I like whisky better, though.

Tokuda Do you cook by yourself?

Young Sometimes I cook myself and sometimes I eat out.

! Notes

1. お慣れになりましたか **"Have you gotten used to …?"**
   Since Mrs. Tokuda is asking about Mr. Young's state of being, she uses the verb 慣れる (get used to) in the honorific お + Vstem + になる pattern.

2. おかげ様で **"thankfully," "thanks to you"**
   The set phrase おかげで, or the politer おかげ様で, expresses gratitude for blessings received or acts of human kindness. The idea is that Mrs. Tokuda and others have been kind to Mr. Young, thus making it easy for him to adjust to Japanese life.

3. めしあがりますか **"Do you eat …?"**
   めしあがる is a special honorific verb meaning "to eat" or "to drink."

4. なさいます？ **"Do you do …?"**

なさる is a special honorific verb for する. Mrs. Tokuda could have used the question-forming particle か after なさいます, but instead she speaks with a rising intonation, making it clear that she is asking a question. Not using か actually makes the question sound softer.

5. です **"do"**

です is used in place of します since the meaning is clear from the context.

Practice

Rewrite the following sentences using the words given.

1. ビルは英語で話したり日本語で話したりします。

→ ヒル先生は＿＿＿＿＿＿＿＿＿＿＿＿＿＿＿＿。

Bill sometimes speaks in English and sometimes speaks in Japanese.

→ Professor Hill ...

2. お兄さん、坂田さんにどこで会うの？

→ 課長、＿＿＿＿＿＿＿＿＿＿＿＿＿＿＿。

Brother, where will you meet Mr. Sakata?

→ Chief, ...?

3. 奥様、この素敵なバッグ、どちらでお買いになったのですか。

→ 安子、＿＿＿＿＿＿＿＿＿＿＿＿＿＿？

Madame, where did you buy this lovely bag?

→ Yasuko, ...?

4. 部長は日本酒も洋酒もめしあがります。

→ 兄は＿＿＿＿＿＿＿＿＿＿＿＿＿＿＿＿。

Our general manager drinks both sake and foreign liquors.

→ My older brother ...

5. 和夫、昨日、美術館で何見たの？

→ 先生、＿＿＿＿＿＿＿＿＿＿＿＿＿＿＿。

Kazuo, what did you see in the art museum yesterday?

→ Professor, ...?

Describing Ongoing and Completed Actions

A Mr. Kubo notices that Ms. Asano is working late, and starts a conversation with her.

37

久保 浅野さん、まだ帰らないんですか。何をしている

んですか。

浅野 明日のミーティングのレポートを準備しているん

です。もうすぐ終わります。

久保 秘書の吉岡さんはもう帰ったんですね。

浅野 まだでしょう。さっき部屋のドアがまだ開いてい

ました。

久保　浅野さんは神戸の出身ですってね。

浅野　ええ。両親は今でも神戸に住んでいますし、弟も

　　　神戸の銀行に勤めています。

久保　そうですか。僕の姉も結婚して、今、神戸に住ん

　　　でいるんですよ。

Kubo　Ms. Asano, you still aren't going home? What are you doing?

Asano　I'm preparing a report for tomorrow's meeting. I'm almost finished.

Kubo　Ms. Yoshioka, the secretary, has already gone home, hasn't she?

Asano　Probably not. A little while ago the door to her office was still open.

Kubo　I hear that you are from Kobe.

Asano　Yes. My parents still live in Kobe, and my younger brother works for a bank there.

Kubo　Really? My older sister got married and now lives in Kobe.

⚠ Notes

1. 何をしているんですか "**What are you doing?**"
   んですか is used when the speaker is asking for an explanation.

2. 準備しているんです "**I am preparing …**"
   Ms. Asano uses んです because she is explaining what she is doing.

3. ですってね "I hear that …," "right?"

The ending ですってね is colloquial for だそうですね, where そうです is used in the pattern S + そうです to convey hearsay (example in Dialogue A, p. 162).

4. 神戸に住んでいますし "lives in Kobe, and …"

The verb 住む (live) expresses a habitual action and is always used in the form 住んでいる, not 住む, when one is talking about someone currently living somewhere.

5. 勤めています "works for," "is working for"

The verb 勤める (work for, be employed) refers to an action repeated for a certain duration of time.

B Yukiko calls Helen in the evening to talk about their plans to see a concert a couple days from now.

38

ヘレン　もしもし。

由紀子　ヘレンさん、私。今忙しい？

ヘレン　ううん、もうご飯も食べ終わって、今お茶を飲みながらテレビを見てるところ。

由紀子　そう。あさってのコンサートは2時半からよ。切符は私が持ってるわ。

ヘレン　どこで会う？

由紀子 コンサートホールは知ってるでしょう？　あの
　　　　ホールの前で2時10分頃待ってるわ。きっと大
　　　　勢集まってるわよ。

ヘレン　じゃあ、その頃行くわ。お電話ありがとう。

由紀子 いいえ。お休みなさい。

Helen　Hello?
Yukiko　Helen, it's me. Are you busy now?
Helen　No, I've already finished eating, and now I'm (in the midst of) watching TV while drinking tea.
Yukiko　I see. The concert the day after tomorrow will start at two thirty. I have the tickets.
Helen　Where do you want to meet?
Yukiko　You know where the concert hall is, don't you? I'll be waiting for you in front of the hall at around 2:10. I'm sure there will be large crowds.
Helen　Then I'll be there around that time. Thanks for calling.
Yukiko　You're welcome. Good night.

⚠ Notes

1. 食べ終わって "finished eating, and …"
食べ終わる is a compound verb consisting of 食べる (eat) and 終わる (be finished). Vstem + 終わる can be applied to virtually any verb to convey the meaning "finish doing something."

2. テレビを見てるところ "I'm (in the midst of) watching TV"

The pattern Vte + (い)るところ expresses an ongoing action. と
ころ (place) is a noun that can mean "moment": *I have finished
eating, and now is the moment I am watching TV while drinking
tea*. It may be followed by です, or by だ if the speaker is male;
without a copula, it is neutral-sounding.

3. 持ってる "have"

持つ (have) is used in the -ている form to indicate the state
of "having." The -ている form is contracted to -てる in casual
conversation.

4. 待ってる / 集まってる "am waiting"/"are gathered"

When these verbs are used in the -ている form (here contracted
to -てる), they indicate a continuous state resulting from a
completed action.

C **Mrs. Sasaki, the pastor's wife, speaks with Ms. Shirai, a
young volunteer, just before a reception at a church hall.**

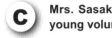

佐々木　白井さん、レセプションの準備はできましたか。

白井　はい、ほとんどできております。

佐々木　いすは十分あるでしょうね。

白井　はい、木田さん達がいすを余分に入れていました。

佐々木　パンフレットはテーブルの上に並べてありますね？

白井　はい、並べてございます。デザートも飲み物も十

分、用意してございます。

佐々木　お花は各テーブルにありますね。

白井　はい、お花は富田さんが用意なさいました。

Sasaki	Ms. Shirai, is everything ready for the reception?
Shirai	Yes, just about.
Sasaki	There are enough chairs, I hope.
Shirai	Yes. Mr. Kida and the others have brought in (lit. put in) more than enough chairs.
Sasaki	The pamphlets are (placed) on the tables, aren't they?
Shirai	Yes, they're there. Plenty of desserts and drinks are also ready.
Sasaki	Each table has flowers, hasn't it?
Shirai	Yes, Mrs. Tomita has taken care of the flowers.

! Notes

1. できております "is ready"

   できております is the humble and polite equivalent of できている, which expresses a state resulting from a previous action.

2. 並べてございます / 用意してございます "are placed"/"have been prepared/readied"

   One of the usages of ございます is as a superpolite auxiliary verb equivalent to いる or ある. The phrases here are superpolite equivalents of 並べてある / 並べてあります and 用意してある / 用意してあります.

3. 用意なさいました "prepared," "took care of"

   なさいました is the past tense of the special honorific verb な

さいます (meaning the same as する). Here it is attached to a noun (用意 preparation) in the N + する pattern.

✎ Practice

Rewrite the following sentences using the words given.

1. 社長のご長男は結婚していらっしゃいます。

   → うちの長男は＿＿＿＿＿＿＿＿＿＿＿＿＿＿。

   The eldest son of the company president is married.

   → Our eldest son …

2. 町田先生は古典文学を研究なさっていらっしゃいます。

   → 私は＿＿＿＿＿＿＿＿＿＿＿＿＿＿。

   Professor Machida is studying classical literature.

   → I …

3. 道子さん、このドア開けてあるの？

   → 課長、＿＿＿＿＿＿＿＿＿＿＿＿＿＿＿。

   Michiko, is this door to be kept open?

   → Chief, …?

4. 父は地下鉄で会社に通っております。

   → 敏子さんのお父様は＿＿＿＿＿＿＿＿＿＿＿＿＿＿＿＿。

   My father is commuting to the company by subway.

   → Toshiko' s father …

5. 小川さん、このデータ直してある？

   → 課長、＿＿＿＿＿＿＿＿＿＿＿＿＿＿＿。

   Mr. Ogawa (coworker), has this data been corrected?

   → Chief, …?

Lesson 9

Stating Reasons

Ms. Yagi notices that Mr. Ono, who is expected to be at a meeting that is about to take place, has not arrived yet, and expresses concern to her colleagues.

40

八木　もう9時過ぎですよ。小野さんはまだ来ませんね。

今朝大事な会議があるのに どうしたんでしょう?

野田　病気じゃないですか。

岡　そんなことはないでしょう。昨日はとても元気で

したから。

野田　もう少し待って、携帯に電話してみます。

八木　まあ、小野さん！　みんな心配<ruby>心配<rt>しんぱい</rt></ruby>していたんですよ。

小野　<ruby>遅<rt>おく</rt></ruby>れてすみません。いやあ、<ruby>信号<rt>しんごう</rt></ruby>の<ruby>故障<rt>こしょう</rt></ruby>で<ruby>電車<rt>でんしゃ</rt></ruby>が

　　　<ruby>1時間以上<rt>じ かん い じょう</rt></ruby>も<ruby>止<rt>と</rt></ruby>まったんですよ。携帯もつながら

　　　ないし、会議があるので<ruby>本当<rt>ほんとう</rt></ruby>にいらいらしましたよ。

Yagi   It's already past nine o'clock. Mr. Ono hasn't come yet.
        What could have happened? There's an important meeting
        this morning.

Noda   Maybe he's sick.

Oka   I don't think so (lit. It's probably not that). He was in great
        spirits yesterday.

Noda   I'll wait a little longer and then call his cell phone (to see
        what is wrong).

Yagi   Oh, Mr. Ono! We were worried about you.

Ono   Sorry for being late. I'm afraid the train stopped for more
        than an hour due to a traffic signal disorder. My cell phone
        wasn't working (lit. would not connect), and since (I knew)
        there was a meeting, I got very irritated.

! Notes

1. 会議があるのに lit. "in spite of the fact that there is a meeting"
   The pattern Vdic + のに is used to connect an action (Vdic)
   with a result (what follows のに) that is contrary to expectation
   or is dissatisfying.

2. どうしたんでしょう？ "What could have happened?"
   どうした？ is used to ask, "What's wrong?" Here the speaker

uses んです in the presumptive form んでしょう because she is asking for an explanation.

3. 電話してみます "call (and see)"
The pattern Vte + みる is used to indicate that someone (the subject of the verb) will try something. Here Mr. Noda will call Mr. Ono to see what is wrong.

4. 心配していたんですよ "We were worried about you"
Again, the speaker uses んです because she is explaining the circumstances. A simple 心配していました would sound unemotional and a little puzzling. ん adds emotion to the sentence, as does the exclamatory よ (didn't you know?).

5. いやあ "I'm afraid …"
いやあ is an interjection used by male speakers when one is embarrassed or shy about something, or when one is surprised to see someone.

6. 止まったんですよ "stopped, you see"
Once again, the speaker is explaining something, so he uses んです.

7. 会議があるので "since/because there is a meeting"
ので indicates an objective reason that has nothing to do with the speaker's opinion or desire. In principle, the ので clause cannot be followed by a main clause involving the speaker's volition or opinion, nor by a command, a request, or an invitation. However, in actual practice it sometimes is.

Mr. Kawase and Ms. Nonaka are at an airport, anxiously waiting for their friend Mr. Yokota, who has not shown up even though the departure time is approaching.

川瀬　あいつ、何してんだろう？　飛行機に乗り遅れるぜ。

野中　おかしいなあ。いつも時間、正確なのに。

川瀬　日を間違えたかな。

野中　まさか！　それほどぼけちゃいないわよ。

川瀬　搭乗が始まったよ。携帯、持ってる？

野中　うん、かけてみるね。呼んでる。出ないな。

川瀬　あっ！　来た、来た。

横田　ごめん、ごめん。本当にすまん。

川瀬　どうしてこんなに遅れたんだ？　心配してたんだぞ。

横田　ゆうべ突然昔の友達が来て飲み過ぎたんだよ。目覚まし時計かけ忘れたんで、今朝、鳴らなかったんだ。

Kawase　What's he doing, I wonder. He's going to miss the plane.

Nonaka　This is out of the ordinary. He's always punctual.

Kawase　I wonder if he got the date messed up.

Nonaka No way! He hasn't gone senile yet.

Kawase They're starting to board. Do you have your cell phone?

Nonaka Yeah, I'll call him and see what's going on. It's ringing. No answer.

Kawase There he is!

Yokota Sorry, sorry. I'm really sorry.

Kawase Why are you so late? We were worried.

Yokota Last night an old buddy showed up (at my place) and we drank too much. I forgot to set the alarm, so it didn't ring this morning.

⚠ Notes

1. あいつ "**he**"

   あいつ (he/she) is often used by male speakers to show hostile or contemptuous feeling toward someone, but in some cases—such as this one—it indicates the speaker's affection for or intimacy with that person.

2. 何してんだろう？ "**What's he doing?**"

   This is a contracted form of 何をしているのだろう?, where のだろう is the presumptive form of のです in the plain style. Once again, ん is used because the speaker is asking for an explanation (at least insofar as he is talking to himself).

3. 乗り遅れるぜ "**He is going to be late boarding (the plane)**"

   乗り遅れる is a compound verb consisting of 乗る (board, get on) and 遅れる (be late). The particle ぜ at the end of the sentence is used by a male speaker toward someone he is close to, to elicit agreement or to give his words emphasis.

4. 時間、正確なのに lit. "**in spite of the fact that he is (always) punctual**"

The pattern Adj + のに is used to connect a state (Adj) with a result (what follows のに) that is contrary to expectation or is dissatisfying. The result in this case (Yokota not showing up) is omitted since it is clear from the context.

5. まさか！ **"No way!" "You've got to be kidding!"**
まさか is an interjection used by both male and female speakers in casual conversation to express surprise. It means that the speaker does not believe or agree with what someone has just said, or does believe it but can't get over it.

6. ぼけちゃいない **"hasn't gone senile"**
ぼけちゃいない is a casual contraction of ぼけてはいない, where ぼけて is the verb ぼける (go senile) in the -て form, followed by a contrastive は and いない.

7. 携帯、持ってる？ **"Do you have your cell phone?"**
Particles are often omitted in casual conversation. Here, the direct-object marker を has been dropped.

8. ごめん / すまん **"sorry"**
Both ごめん and すまん are used for apology in casual conversation—ごめん by both male and female speakers, and すまん only by male speakers. すまん is a contraction of すまない, which is the plain-style form of すみません.

9. どうしてこんなに遅れたんだ？ **"Why are you so late?"**
こんなに is a contraction of このように (in this way, to this extent). んだ？ as a question is used by male speakers in casual conversation with friends or family. The speaker is asking for an explanation, which is why he uses んだ？

10. 心配してたんだぞ "We were worried"

心配してた is a contraction of 心配していた. The speaker uses んだ because he is explaining the circumstances. ぞ at the end is a particle used by a male speaker to state with emphasis his feeling or judgment.

11. かけ忘れたんで "because I forgot to set (the alarm clock)"

This is the casual equivalent of かけ忘れたので, where ので indicates a reason. かけ忘れる is a compound verb consisting of かける (set) and 忘れる (forget).

Mr. Kaji, a young employee, is at a banquet and is concerned about the absence of his boss, the subsection chief, so he asks the section chief about him.

梶 (かじ)　課長、三輪係長はなぜ今晩の宴会に出席されな

かったんですか。

課長　明日の朝早い新幹線で大阪へ行くからだろう。

梶　また大阪へ出張されるんですか。

課長　うん。君も例の岩井物産の件は知ってるね。

梶　はい、存じております。詳しいことはうかがって

おりませんが。

課長　あの件で、ちょっとトラブルが起こってね。

梶　それで、大阪にはどのくらい滞在されるんですか。

課長　1週間ぐらいだろう。ところで、これからどこか

で一杯やるんだが、君もどうだね？

梶　申し訳ございませんが、今晩はちょっと……。実

は、ゆうべ両親が上京しまして待っておりますので。

Kaji	Chief, why didn't Subsection Chief Miwa attend tonight's banquet?
Chief	Probably because he's going to Osaka tomorrow morning on an early bullet train.
Kaji	Another business trip to Osaka?
Chief	Yes. You, too, know about that deal with Iwai Trading Company, don't you?
Kaji	Yes, I know. I haven't heard the details, though.
Chief	There's been some trouble.
Kaji	Then how long will he stay in Osaka?
Chief	Probably about a week. By the way, we are going out for some drinks now (lit. from now, we are going to have a drink somewhere). How about you?
Kaji	I'm very sorry, but tonight isn't the best time…. Actually, my parents came up to Tokyo last night and are waiting for me.

❗ Notes

1. なぜ "why"

The interrogative adverb なぜ is used to inquire about a reason or cause. It is more formal than どうして.

2. 出席されなかったんですか "didn't ... attend?"

出席されなかった is the negative past tense of 出席される, which is the passive form of 出席する used for the honorific style. Notice that Mr. Kaji uses んですか to ask about the circumstances of the subsection chief's absence.

3. 出張される "go on a business trip"

出張される is 出張する in the passive form used for the honorific style.

4. 例の "that (deal)"

例の is used to indicate a topic that the speaker and listener recently discussed or both know about.

5. 存じております "I know"

The special humble verb 存じる (know) is always used in the -ている form to describe a state of knowing. 存じております is more humble than 存じています (because of the おります) and much more humble than 知っています.

6. うかがっております "I haven't heard"

うかがう (hear) is a special humble verb. うかがっておりません is more humble than うかがっていません and much more humble than 聞いていません.

7. 起こってね "has occurred, and ..."

This is an example of ellipsis (the omission of unneeded words) in Japanese. Between て and ね there is an implied verb, but this is enough for the chief to get his idea across—he doesn't need to say anything more.

8. 滞在される "stay"

滞在される is 滞在する in the passive form used for the honorific style.

9. どこか "somewhere"

An interrogative pronoun followed by か changes the word into what in English would be an indefinite pronoun or adverb: どこ (where) + か = somewhere/anywhere; 何 (what) + か = something/anything; だれ (who) + か = someone/anyone; etc.

10. 一杯やるんだが "we are going out for some drinks"

一杯やる (have a drink) is a useful word to know. Consisting of the noun 一杯 (one glass; drinking a little alcohol) and the verb やる (do), it does not necessarily mean to drink only one glass of alcohol; more often than not, it means to drink several. のですが, or in this case the plain-style んだが, is used when the speaker is bringing up a new subject and needs to provide some background information first.

11. 申し訳ございません "sorry," lit. "I have no excuse"

This is a formal and polite way of apologizing.

12. 今晩はちょっと…… "Tonight isn't the best time.…"

ちょっと (a little) is used here as a softener, cushioning the impact of what is about to be said. In fact, this is all Mr. Kaji needs to say to convey that tonight is no good. The 〜はちょっと pattern is often used in this way to politely decline an invitation.

13. 待っております "are waiting"

This is the humble equivalent of 待っています.

Practice

Correct the speech-style mistakes in the following sentences.

1. お客様はまだいらっしゃらないのですか。どうしたんだろう？

The guests haven't come yet? What happened to them?

2. 課長、車が途中で故障したんで会議に遅れたんだ。本当にすまん。

Chief, I was late for the meeting because my car broke down on the way. I'm terribly sorry.

3. 上司の川田さんが京都へ出張したから、私が代わりに宴会に出席されたんです。

My boss, Mr. Kawada, went on a business trip to Kyoto, so I attended the banquet in his place.

4. 伊豆で、田中さん夫婦がそのホテルに滞在したので、私達ご夫婦も同じホテルに滞在されたんです。

Mr. and Mrs. Tanaka (the Tanaka couple) stayed at that hotel in Izu, so we (my wife and I) also stayed there.

5. 「サンドラさん、小野田先生はもう帰りましたか」

「いいえ、前の学生が来られたから、今、職員室で話しております」

"Sandra, has Professor Onoda already gone home?"

"No, his former student came, so he's in his office talking with her."

Inviting, Suggesting, and Advising

 A

Ms. Oki, who works at the school office, invites Maria, a new student, to the Gion Festival parade.

43

沖 マリアさん、土曜日に何か予定がありますか。

マリア いいえ、別に。何か面白いこと、ないでしょうか。

沖 今、京都で祇園祭をやっていますよ。

マリア そうらしいですね。パレードがあるんですか。

沖 ええ、豪華に飾った車のパレードです。京都の有名な行事ですから、大勢の人が見に来ます。一緒に見に行きましょうか。

マリア　ええ、よろこんで。

沖　　とても暑いから、帽子をかぶって行ったほうがいいですよ。

マリア　ジャネットさんも誘いませんか。きっと喜びます。

沖　　ええ、ぜひそうしましょう。

Oki	Maria, do you have any plans for Saturday?
Maria	No, not particularly. Is there anything interesting going on? (lit. Is there nothing interesting?)
Oki	The Gion Festival is going on in Kyoto right now.
Maria	So it would seem. Is there a parade?
Oki	Yes, it's a parade of gorgeously decorated carriages. It's a famous event in Kyoto, so many people come to see it. Do you want to go see it together?
Maria	Yes, I'd love to.
Oki	It's going to be very hot, so we'd better go with hats on.
Maria	Wouldn't you (like to) invite Janet, too? She'd surely be happy (to be invited).
Oki	Yes, by all means let's do so.

! Notes

1. そうらしいですね "So it would seem"

らしい at the end of a sentence indicates the speaker's belief or understanding about something (the statement that comes before らしい) based on reliable information or objective observation. It is used in the pattern N + らしい or plain-style verb/

i-adjective + らしい; when a na-adjective comes before らしい, the stem is used (e.g. 上手^{じょう ず}らしい).

2. 見に "to see"

The pattern Vstem + に indicates a purpose when the verb that follows is directional. Directional verbs include 来^くる (come), 行く (go), 出^でかける (go out), 帰^{かえ}る (return), and 入^{はい}る (enter), among others.

3. よろこんで "with pleasure"

Both the -ましょう form (e.g. 行きましょう) and the phrase よろこんで (with pleasure) can be used to accept an invitation.

4. 帽子をかぶって行ったほうがいい "had better go with a hat on"

The pattern Vta + ほうがいい is used to advise someone to do something. In place of the -た form, the dictionary form may also be used: かぶって行くほうがいい.

5. 誘いませんか "Wouldn't you (like to) invite …?"

誘いませんか is the negative form of 誘いましょうか. Both phrases express a first-person invitation or suggestion. The negative form is more polite, showing more consideration for the listener, who may wish to give a negative answer.

 B **Mr. Takahashi, a company employee, talks Mr. Brown, his coworker, into going out for dinner.**

高橋^{たかはし} 明日^{あした}の晩^{ばん}、ひま？

ブラウン うん、ひまだよ。特^{とく}に予定^{よ てい}ない。

高橋　じゃあ、すしでも食べに行こうか？

ブラウン　どこへ行く？

高橋　この前、課長のおごりで銀座のすし屋へ行った

んだよ。うまかったぞ。そこへ行こう。

ブラウン　いいね。すしは大好物だよ。

高橋　ハリスさんも誘わないか？　彼も日本食は好き

なんだろう？

ブラウン　いや、彼、すしとさしみは苦手なんだよ。納豆さ

え食べるのにな。

高橋　そうか。じゃあ、今回は彼に言わないほうがいいな。

Takahashi	Are you free tomorrow evening?
Brown	Yeah, I'm free. No particular plans.
Takahashi	Then shall we go out for sushi or something?
Brown	Where to?
Takahashi	The other day we went to a sushi shop in Ginza on the section chief's treat. It was excellent. Let's go there.
Brown	Good idea. Sushi is my favorite food.
Takahashi	Wouldn't you (like to) invite Mr. Harris, too? He too likes Japanese food, doesn't he?
Brown	No, he doesn't like sushi and sashimi. Though he does eat *natto* (fermented soybeans), believe it or not.
Takahashi	Really? Then we'd better not say anything to him this time.

⚠ Notes

1. 明日の晩、ひま？ "Are you free tomorrow evening?"

Mr. Takahashi omits です か after ひ ま (free time) because this is casual conversation and Mr. Brown is someone with whom he does not have to use the polite style.

2. 特に予定ない "No particular plans"

This is another case of a speaker omitting particles. The omitted particle here is は: 特に予定はない.

3. すしでも "sushi or something"

The pattern N + でも is used to casually mention something as a suggestion.

4. 行こうか？ "Shall we go?"

The pattern Vvol + か is used to express a first-person invitation or suggestion. It is used mostly by male speakers in casual conversation.

5. 行こう "Let's go"

行こう is the volitional form of 行く and the casual equivalent of 行きましょう.

6. 誘わないか？ "Wouldn't you (like to) invite …?"

誘わないか？ is the casual equivalent of 誘いませんか.

7. 好きなんだろう？ "likes …, doesn't (he)?"

なんだろう？ is んだ with だ in the presumptive form; ん becomes なん because what precedes it is a na-adjective. なんだろう？ (spoken with a rising intonation) is used by male speakers for confirmation in casual conversation.

8. 納豆さえ "even *natto*"

The pattern N + さえ is used to cite an extreme or unexpected example.

9. 言わないほうがいい "had better not say"

The pattern Vneg + ないほうがいい is used to advise someone not to do something.

C Two female students, Midori and Asako, wish to have Professor Miller at a party Asako is having at her house. Asako tries to persuade him to come.

45

みどり 明日のパーティーにミラー先生をお招きしたらどう?

朝子 そうねえ。お話ししてみましょうか。

みどり そうしたほうがいいわよ。

＊　＊　＊

朝子 先生、明日の午後、私の家でパーティーをしますが、いらっしゃいませんか。日本の食べ物や飲み物をたくさん準備しています。

ミラー ありがとう、でも明日はちょっと……。2時に友人の画家の個展に 行くんです。

朝子　パーティーは5時頃まで続きますから、お帰りにちょっとお寄りになったらどうでしょうか。

ミラー　じゃあ、あまり遅くならないほうがいいから、4時頃うかがいましょうか。

朝子　わかりました。お待ちしております。ここに私の住所と電話番号と地図がございます。どうぞ。

Midori	How about inviting Professor Miller to tomorrow's party?
Asako	Good idea. Shall I speak to him and see?
Midori	I think you ought to.

* * *

Asako	Professor, we will have a party at my house tomorrow afternoon. Wouldn't you (like to) come? We are preparing plenty of Japanese food and drinks.
Miller	Thank you, but tomorrow isn't the best time…. I'm going to an exhibition by a painter friend of mine at two o'clock.
Asako	The party will continue until around five, so how about stopping by for just a little while on your way back?
Miller	In that case, it's best not to be too late, so shall I come around four?
Asako	Okay. We'll be waiting for you. Here's my address and phone number, and a map. Please take it.

! Notes

1. お招きしたらどう？ "How about inviting …?"

The pattern Vtara + どう？ is used for a suggestion or an invi-

tation in casual conversation. お招きする is the humble form of
招く (invite).

2. いらっしゃいませんか **"Wouldn't you (like to) come?"**
This is the honorific equivalent of 来ませんか.

3. 個展に **"to an exhibition"**
The pattern N (activity) + に indicates a purpose with directional verbs such as 行く or 来る. Some examples of activity
nouns are 買い物 (shopping), 仕事 (work), and 散歩 (walk). 個
展 is an exhibition by a single artist rather than one by several.

4. 行くんです **"am going (to …)"**
Professor Miller uses the polite style throughout this conversation because he and Asako are not that close. They are teacher
and student, a relationship that usually requires a more cour-
teous style than, say, a boss and an employee working under
him.

5. どうでしょうか **"How about …?"**
どうでしょうか is a politer way of saying どうですか.

6. うかがいましょうか **"Shall I come?"**
うかがいましょうか is the humble equivalent of 行きましょうか.
Although Professor Miller is of higher social standing than
Asako, he uses the humble form here because he is graciously
responding to Asako's invitation. Japanese people usually use
humble forms in situations like this, regardless of their social
status.

7. お待ちしております **"will be waiting"**
This is the humble equivalent of 待っています.

Practice

A. Answer the following invitations or suggestions positively and negatively.

1. トム、今晩、映画を見に行かない？

   Tom, shall we go to see the movie tonight?

   → _____。

   → _____。

2. 正子さん、帰りにスーパーに寄って買い物をしませんか。

   Masako, shall we stop by the supermarket on the way home and do some shopping?

   → _____。

   → _____。

3. 先生、私達のピクニックにいらっしゃいませんか。

   Professor, wouldn't you like to come to our picnic?

   → _____。

   → _____。

B. Give the following suggestions or advice to the person indicated in parentheses.

1. tidy up (片付ける) the room   (your younger brother)

2. not reply (返事する) now   (a coworker)

3. invite Mr. Yamagishi to play golf   (your superior)

Lesson 11

Making Requests

A Ms. Hatano, the deputy section chief, comes to Ms. Minami, a junior clerk, to ask her to do some work.

46

畑野　南さん、このレポートの間違いを直してください。

　　　赤線が引いてありますから、すぐわかりますよ。

南　　お急ぎですか。

畑野　そうですねえ。課長が九州から帰るまでにお願い

　　　します。

南　　わかりました。課長のお帰りはあさってですね。

畑野　ええ。それで、この仕事を済ませてから林さんの
　　　プロジェクトを手伝ってください。

南　　はい。ついでですが、この箱の中の古い書類は捨
　　　てましょうか。

畑野　いいえ、それはまだ捨てないでください。

Hatano　Ms. Minami, please correct the mistakes in this report. The mistakes are underlined in red, so you'll find them easily.

Minami　Are you in a hurry?

Hatano　Sort of. I'd like you to get it done before the section chief returns from Kyushu.

Minami　Certainly, ma'am. He'll return the day after tomorrow, won't he?

Hatano　Yes. And after you have finished this job, please help Mr. Hayashi with his project.

Minami　Okay. By the way, shall I throw away these old papers in this box?

Hatano　No, don't throw them away yet.

⚠ Notes

1. 直してください "Please correct …"

   The pattern Vte + ください is used to convey a polite request to an equal or a subordinate. It should not be used toward superiors.

2. 帰るまでに "before he returns"

   The pattern Vdic + までに is used to indicate a limit or deadline for an action or request expressed in the main clause (the clause that follows).

3. 済ませてから "after you have finished"

The pattern Vte + から is used to express a time relationship (after, since) between actions.

4. 捨てないでください "Please don't throw … away"

The pattern Vneg + ないでください is used to express a negative request.

B Returning home, a father finds his wife trying to put away several big packages that have just been delivered, and calls on his sons to help.

47

母　あ、あなた、お帰りなさい。ちょっとこれ持って！

父　重いな。どこに置くんだ？

母　とりあえず、そのテーブルの上に置いて。中身は壊れ物だから気をつけて。

父　一人で大変だなあ。子供達は？

母　2階で何かやってるわ。

父　おい、お前達！　早く降りてきて、お母さんを手伝いなさい。

兄　わかった、すぐ行くよ。おい、孝夫、止めろよそのパソコン。お父さんが呼んでるよ。

弟　　このゲーム、もうすぐ終わるんだ。もうちょっと

　　　待ってよ。

兄　　止めろったら！　お父さん怒るぞ。

弟　　わかったよ。そんなにがみがみ言うなよ。

Mother	Oh, welcome home, dear. Hold this, please!
Father	It's heavy. Where should I put it?
Mother	For the time being, put it on that table. The contents are fragile, so be careful.
Father	Must have been hard for you (to handle these) by yourself. Where are the kids?
Mother	They're upstairs, doing something.
Father	Hey, kids! Quick, come down here and help your mother.
Older Brother	Okay, coming. Hey, Takao, quit the computer. Dad is calling us.
Younger Brother	This game will be finished in a sec. Wait, will you?
Older Brother	Quit, I said! Dad is going to get mad!
Younger Brother	Okay. Don't yell at me like that.

! Notes

1. これ持って！ "Hold this!"

   The -て form by itself (without ください) can be used to convey a casual request to a family member or friend.

2. 子供達は？ "The kids?"

   The father omits the question, Where are they? because it is obvious that that is what he means. Another example of ellipsis.

3. おい "hey"

おい is used by male speakers in rough speech to get attention.

4. 降りてきて "come down here and ..."

The pattern Vte + くる / いく is used to indicate the direction of the action expressed by the verb. くる (come) in this position indicates an action moving toward the speaker, and いく (go) an action that moves away from him. The father is at the bottom of the stairs, so he yells to his kids to come down; if he were at the top of the stairs with his kids and telling them to go down, he would use 降りていって.

5. 手伝いなさい "Help her"

Vstem + なさい is used by teachers or parents when speaking to their students or children to express a plain-style command.

6. 止めろよ "Quit"

止めろ is the imperative (command) form of the regular II verb 止める (quit) and is used by male speakers in rough speech. The particle よ may be added to 止めろ for emphasis.

7. 待ってよ "Wait"

This is the -て form and is used toward friends and family members to convey a casual request. Had Takao wanted to command his older brother to wait, he would have used the imperative form of 待つ, which is 待て. The imperative form of regular I verbs follows this pattern, where the final syllable ends with an "e" sound. The particle よ may be added to either the -て form or the imperative form for emphasis.

8. 止めろったら！ "Quit!"

止めろ + たら becomes 止めろったら in a pattern that is used to emphasize a repeated command.

9. 言うなよ "Don't yell"

The pattern Vdic + な is used by male speakers in rough speech to tell someone in very strong words not to do something. よ can be added for emphasis.

C After class, Jeff comes to the teachers' office, where Ms. Mikami and Mr. Sano are in. He asks Ms. Mikami, his teacher, to lend him a dictionary.

48

三上　ああ、ジェフさん、まだいたんですか。<u>何かご用？</u>

ジェフ　今教室で宿題をしています。先生、すみませんが<u>辞書を貸してくださいませんか。</u>

三上　いいですよ。これを<u>お使いなさい。</u>学校を出る前に<u>返してくださいね。</u>

ジェフ　はい、必ず<u>お返しいたします。</u>ありがとうございました。

三上　<u>あら、</u>佐野先生、もう<u>お帰りですか。</u>

佐野　いや、これから図書館へ本を返しに寄って、ミーティングに出るんですよ。あとでこの<u>窓を閉めていただけませんか。</u>

三上　はい。あ、その文法の本はまだ返さないでいただ

けませんか。明日、学生に見せますから。

Mikami　Oh, Jeff, you're still here? How can I help you?

Jeff　I'm in the classroom doing my homework now. Sorry to bother you, but would you please lend me a dictionary?

Mikami　All right. Use this. But return it to me before you leave school, okay?

Jeff　Yes, I will certainly return it. Thank you.

Mikami　Oh, Sano-sensei, are you going home now?

Sano　No, I'm going to the library to return these books, and then I'm going to attend a meeting. Would you mind closing these windows later?

Mikami　Sure. Oh, would you please not return that grammar book yet? I plan on showing it to my students tomorrow.

！ Notes

1. 何かご用？ lit. "Some business (here)?"

用 means "something to do," "business," etc., and is used here in the polite form ご用. Ms. Mikami leaves out the rest of the question because this phrase is enough to make herself understood, and 何かご用ですか would sound too direct.

2. 貸してくださいませんか "Please lend me …"

The pattern Vte + くださいませんか is used to convey a polite request to a superior.

3. お使いなさい "Use (this)"

The honorific prefix お- is added to a verb in the Vstem + な

さい pattern (Note 5, p. 117) to make a plain-style command sound a little politer, a little softer.

4. お返しいたします "**will return it**"
This is the humble equivalent of 返します.

5. あら "**oh**"
あら is used by female speakers to express surprise.

6. 閉めていただけませんか "**Would you mind closing …?**"
The pattern Vte + いただけませんか is used toward superiors to convey a very polite request and is a little more polite than Vte + くださいませんか. いただけませんか by itself means "Could I receive …?"

7. 返さないでいただけませんか "**Would you please not return …?**"
The pattern Vneg + ないでいただけませんか is used toward superiors to convey a very polite negative request.

✏️ Practice

Make the following requests to the person indicated in parentheses.

1. to check (調べる) the data before the meeting starts (始まる)
(a coworker)

2. not to park (駐車する) here (a customer)

3. to play after finishing homework (your son)

4. not to enter (入る) that room (a visitor)

5. to show (見せる) you that photo (写真) (your friend)

Expressing Ability

A

49

Mrs. Abe praises Scott, her son Tatsuya's friend, for his ability to speak Japanese.

阿部　スコットさんは日本語がとてもお上手ね。感心し

ているのよ。

スコット　いいえ、まだ下手です。話すことは面白いですが、

読むことは難しいです。書くのはもっと大変です。

阿部　漢字は書けるの？

スコット　ええ、やっと少し書けるようになりました。

阿部 偉いわねえ。うちの達也は外国語はさっぱりだめ

なのよ。

スコット 達也君は柔道が得意ですよ。僕、いつも負けて

います。

Abe	You are very good at Japanese. I'm impressed.
Scott	No, I'm still bad at it. Speaking is fun, but reading is hard. Writing is even harder.
Abe	Can you write kanji?
Scott	Yes, I am finally able to write some (lit. I have finally reached the point where I can write a few).
Abe	How admirable. My son Tatsuya isn't good at any foreign languages.
Scott	Tatsuya is good at judo. I always lose to him.

❗ Notes

1. 話すこと / 読むこと "speaking"/"reading"

こと added to a verb makes the verb into a gerund. Here it refers to the act of speaking and the act of reading.

2. 書くの "writing"

の added to a verb makes the verb into a gerund. の and こと are sometimes but not always interchangeable (see Note 2, p. 124). In this case, they can be interchanged.

3. 書けるの？ "Can you write?"

書ける (can write) is one of two potential forms of 書く. The other is 書くことができる. These two forms are basically interchangeable, though the former is more colloquial.

4. 書けるようになりました **lit. "I have reached the point where I am able to write"**

The pattern Vdic + ようになる expresses a change that gradually takes place.

5. うちの達也 **"my/our son Tatsuya"**

うち means "family" or "household," and here Mrs. Abe uses it to mean her own family. Scott already knows that Tatsuya is her son, of course, so Mrs. Abe's reason for using うちの達也 instead of simply 達也 may not be clear. In fact, うちの helps to establish a contrast between Scott and Tatsuya, and one can read in it Mrs. Abe's emotion. Here うちの is almost demeaning, but de-elevating one's own family when speaking to others is normal and appropriate in Japanese social interaction.

B **Two female workers, Noriko and Hisako, are gossiping about their superiors.**

50

典子　ヒルさんは日本の歌がうまいのよ。この前のパーティーで、彼が歌うのを聞いて驚いたわ。

久子　どこで覚えたのかしら？

典子　多分カラオケよ。彼、輸出部の三宅課長と付き合ってるから。

久子　課長も歌えるの？

典子　ええ、彼、飲めるし、歌えるし。あの二人、テキ

サスの大学で一緒だったのよ。

久子　<u>どうりで課長、日本人にしては英語がよくできる</u>

のね。

Noriko　Mr. Hill is good at (singing) Japanese songs. I heard him singing at the party the other day and was so surprised.

Hisako　Where did he learn how to do it, I wonder.

Noriko　Probably singing karaoke. He often goes out with Mr. Miyake, chief of the export section.

Hisako　Can the section chief sing, too?

Noriko　Yes, he can drink and sing. Those two went to school together at a university in Texas, you know.

Hisako　No wonder the section chief can speak English so well for a Japanese.

⚠ Notes

1. うまい "good," "skillful"

   This うまい, meaning "good" or "skillful," is used in casual conversation by both male and female speakers. See also Note 6, p. 67.

2. 歌うの "singing"

   の indicates the act or instance of Mr. Hill's singing. の is attached to actions the speaker feels close to or empathetic toward. In this case, Noriko saw Mr. Hill singing at a party, so she uses の. If she were talking about singing in an abstract way, she would use こと, as in 歌うことは楽^{たの}しい (singing is fun).

3. 歌える "can sing"

This is a potential form of 歌う (sing). It is used in place of 歌う
ことができる.

4. どうりで "no wonder …"

どうりで is used to express satisfaction when one discovers the
reason for something that has been puzzling one.

5. 日本人にしては "for a Japanese person"

The pattern N + にしては is used to present a standard for
comparisons.

6. 英語ができる "can speak English"

This is short for 英語を話^{はな}すことができる. When a verb is
closely associated with its direct object, the middle part—in
this case, を話すこと (the act of speaking …)—can be omitted.

**Ms. Sato, a young office clerk, asks Ms. Oka, the executive
secretary, about Mr. Wright, the new head of the foreign
department of their company.**

佐藤^{さとう}　新任^{しんにん}のライト部長^{ぶちょう}は日本語^{にほんご}がおできになりますか。

岡^{おか}　ええ、もちろん。日本語でスピーチをなさること
がお得意^{とくい}ですよ。レセプションでお聞^ききしたわ。
中国語^{ちゅうごくご}もお話^{はな}しになれるのよ。

佐藤　ライトさんは日本は初(はじ)めてじゃないのでしょう？

岡　東京(とうきょう)の大学(だいがく)を卒業(そつぎょう)なさってから、しばらくこちら
　　でお仕事(しごと)をしていらしたの。

佐藤　そうなんですか。奥様(おくさま)はどんな方(かた)なんですか。

岡　ブロンドで細(ほそ)い方。アメリカで小学校(しょうがっこう)の先生(せんせい)をな
　　さっていたんですって。

佐藤　じゃあ、日本の子供達(こどもたち)に英語(えいご)を教(おし)えることがおで
　　きになりますね。

岡　さあ。お子(こ)さんが3人(にん)いらっしゃるから、きっと
　　お忙(いそが)しいでしょう。

Sato　Can Mr. Wright, the new general manager, speak Japanese?

Oka　Yes, of course. He is good at making speeches in Japanese. I
　　heard him (speak Japanese) at the reception. He can speak
　　Chinese, too.

Sato　This isn't Mr. Wright's first visit to Japan, is it?

Oka　After graduating from college in Tokyo, he worked (lit. was
　　working) here for some time.

Sato　Really? What kind of person is Mrs. Wright?

Oka　She's blond and thin. In America, she worked (lit. was
　　working) as an elementary school teacher.

Sato　Then she can teach English to Japanese children, can't she?

Oka   Well, she has three children, so I imagine she's (too) busy (for that).

! Notes

1. おできになります "can"
   This is the honorific form of できる (can) in the polite style.

2. スピーチをなさる "make a speech"
   This is the honorific form of スピーチをする (make a speech).

3. お聞きした "heard"
   This is the humble form of 聞いた (heard) in the polite style.

4. お話しになれる "can speak"
   This is the honorific form of the potential verb 話せる (can speak) and an alternative form of お話しになることができる.

5. 卒業なさってから "after graduating"
   This is the honorific equivalent of 卒業してから.

6. お仕事をしていらした "was working"
   The ending いらした is an alternative form of いらっしゃった that is often preferred by female speakers for the softer sound. Both are honorific forms of いた.

7. 先生をなさっていた "was a teacher"
   This is the honorific equivalent of 先生をしていた.

8. お忙しい "is busy"
   The polite prefix お- here is honorific because Ms. Oka is talking about Mr. Wright's wife.

✏️ Practice

What would you say in the following situations?

1. You want to ask your friend's young son, Hiroshi, if he can swim (泳ぐ).

2. You want to tell your friend's mother that reading Japanese is easy but writing it is hard.

3. You want to ask your classmate Sam if he can teach English to Japanese friends.

4. You want to tell your teacher that you cannot translate (訳す) this sentence (文).

5. You want to ask the section chief if the general manager is good at speaking Chinese.

6. You, a young mother, want to tell your friend Tomoko that your baby (子) has started walking.

7. You want to tell your boss that your father cannot drive (運転する) a car.

8. You want to ask your superior's wife if she can make sukiyaki.

9. You want to ask your sister if you can buy a concert ticket (チケット) at the hall (ホール).

Expressing Desire

A A teacher at a Japanese language school asks her students what they want to do during winter break.

先生 皆さん、冬休みはどんな予定ですか。

ビル 僕は車がほしいから、アルバイトをします。

サラ 私は国に帰って、家族と一緒にクリスマスを祝い

たいです。

リサ 私はおじが日本の切手をほしがっているから、で

きるだけたくさん集めてみます。

トム　私は弟が日本に来たがっているから、こちらに呼んで一緒に何かやりたいです。

ジム　僕は何もしたくないです。ただゆっくり眠りたいです。先生は？

先生　先生は皆さんに来学期もがんばってほしいので、授業の準備をします。

Teacher	Everybody, what are your plans for winter break?
Bill	I want a car, so I'm going to work (to save for one).
Sarah	I want to go back to my country and celebrate Christmas with my family.
Lisa	My uncle wants Japanese stamps, so I'm going to try collecting as many as I can.
Tom	My younger brother wants to come to Japan, so I want to invite him to come here and do something together.
Jim	I don't want to do anything. I just want to sleep. Sensei, how about you?
Teacher	Because I want you all to study hard next term, I am going to prepare lessons.

⚠ Notes

1. アルバイト "side job"
   アルバイト is a side job that students or workers take alongside their studies or regular work.

2. 切手をほしがっている lit. "shows signs of wanting stamps"

The pattern Adj stem + がる / がっている is used to express a third person's feeling or thinking a certain way. When がる / がっている attaches to the i-adjective ほしい (want), for example, it expresses someone's desire to have something. In this pattern, the wanted item is marked by the particle を.

3. 来たがっている lit. "shows signs of wanting to come"

The pattern Vstem + たがる / たがっている is used to express a third person's desire to do something.

4. 皆さんに……がんばってほしいので "Because I want you all to study hard …"

The pattern N (person) + に + Vte + ほしい expresses the speaker's desire to have someone (marked by に) do something. Earlier I pointed out (Note 7, p. 95) that ので is mostly used to give objective reasons that have nothing to do with the speaker's desire, but here the teacher uses it to make her wish (that her students study hard next term) the reason for what she says she will do (prepare lessons over the break). Strictly speaking, から would be the more grammatical word choice, but Japanese people sometimes avoid から and use ので instead when they want to make a subjective reason sound softer and politer.

B A mother tries to persuade her young son to stay with his grandparents while she and her husband spend Christmas in Hawaii.

母_{はは}　武夫_{たけお}、クリスマスのプレゼントに何_{なに}がほしい？

何_{なん}でもほしい物_{もの}、言_いってごらんなさい。

131

息子 　僕、何もいらないよ。だってディズニーランドへ
　　　　行きたいもの。

母　　 ディズニーランドもいいけど……。そういえば、
　　　　北海道のおじいちゃんとおばあちゃんが、あなた
　　　　にとても会いたがっているのよ。クリスマスにぜ
　　　　ひ来てほしいんだって。

息子 　北海道？　スキーできるね。

母　　 ええ、スキーもできるし、雪だるまも作れるし
　　　　……。面白いわよ。

息子 　うん、ママも来るんでしょう？

母　　 ママとパパは、今年はハワイでクリスマスを過ご
　　　　したいの。

息子 　ハワイ？　僕も行きたい！　連れてって！　連れ
　　　　てってたら！！

Mother　Takeo, what do you want for Christmas? Name anything
　　　　you want.
Child　　I don't need anything. I want to go to Disneyland.
Mother　Disneyland would be nice.... By the way, Grandpa and

Grandma in Hokkaido really want to see you. They say they really want you to come (to their place) for Christmas.

Child   Hokkaido? I can go skiing, can't I?

Mother Yes, you can ski and you can make a snowman.... It will be fun.

Child   Hmm, you're coming too, aren't you, Mama?

Mother Mama and Papa want to spend this Christmas in Hawaii.

Child   Hawaii? I want to go, too! Take me! Take me, please!

⚠ Notes

1. 何がほしい？ **"What do you want?"**
This is a casual equivalent of 何がほしいですか.

2. 言ってごらんなさい **"Say/Name it"**
This is a politer, softer equivalent of the plain-style command 言ってみなさい. The Vte + ごらんなさい pattern is used toward children or students.

3. だって……行きたいもの **lit. "because I want to go"**
The conjunction だって is used in casual argument when offering a reason or excuse, particularly when the speaker anticipates opposition from the other party. It is often used together with the sentence-final particle もの (or the more colloquial もん), also indicating a reason. The combination of だって and もの / もん is used most often by young women and children when speaking to intimates and carries a sugary tone.

4. 来てほしいんだって **"they want you to come, they say"**
This is a casual equivalent of 来てほしいのですって or 来てほしいのだそうです. だって, って, and だそうだ are all used to quote another person's words.

5. 連れてって！連れてってたら!! "Take me! Take me, please!"
This is a contraction of 連れていって, the casual form of the request 連れていってください (please take me). 連れてってたら！expresses a desperate plea.

C Mr. Miki, a young employee, comes to see the general manager, but finds him tied up with visitors. So he talks with his secretary instead.

54

三木 あのう、部長にお目にかかりたいのですが。

秘書 今、来客中なんですよ。ちょっと時間がかかると思いますが。

三木 じゃあ、部長にこの書類を渡してくださいませんか。明日の会議の前に読んでいただきたいので。

秘書 はい、わかりました。それから、三木さんはいつ休暇をおとりになるの？

三木 来週とりたいと思っています。

秘書 どこかへいらっしゃるんですか。

三木 はい。伊豆温泉へでも。

秘書 まあ、うらやましいわ！

三木　両親が行きたがっておりますので。私はただのお
　　　供なんですよ。

Miki	Uh, I would like to see the general manager.
Secretary	He is having visitors right now. I think it will take some time.
Miki	Well, would you please hand this document to him? I'd like him to read it before tomorrow's meeting.
Secretary	Yes, I will. By the way, Mr. Miki, when are you going to take your vacation?
Miki	I'm thinking of taking next week off.
Secretary	Are you going anywhere?
Miki	Yes. Perhaps to an Izu hot springs.
Secretary	Oh, I'm envious!
Miki	My parents want to go. I am just their companion.

⚠ Notes

1. お目にかかりたい "I would like to see …"
   お目にかかりたい expresses a desire to see or meet one's superior. お目にかかる is a special humble form of the verb 会う (see, meet).

2. と思います "I think …"
   と思います added to a sentence makes it sound less blunt or domineering.

3. （部長に）読んでいただきたい "I would like (the general manager) to read it"
   The pattern N (person) + に + Vte + いただきたい expresses the speaker's desire to have a superior (marked by に) do something for him.

4. とりたいと思っています "I'm thinking of taking …"
   とりたいと思っています sounds softer and politer than とりたいです.

5. 行きたがっております lit. "show signs of wanting to go"
   This is the humble equivalent of 行きたがっています.

✎ Practice

Complete the following sentences.

1. ジョンは日本人（にほんじん）のガールフレンドを_____。
   John wants a Japanese girlfriend.

2. 私（わたし）は母（はは）に_____。
   I want to see my mother.

3. 私は白（しろ）いセーターが_____が、妹（いもうと）は赤（あか）いのを

   _____。

   I want a white sweater, but my younger sister wants a red one.

4. 私はこの本（ほん）を友達（ともだち）の信子（のぶこ）さんに_____。
   I want my friend Nobuko to read this book.

5. ネルソン先生（せんせい）は歌舞伎（かぶき）を_____。
   Professor Nelson wants to see Kabuki.

6. 僕（ぼく）、何（なに）も_____。 ハワイに _____!
   I don't want anything. Take me to Hawaii!

7. 私は先生にこの手紙（てがみ）を_____。
   I would like my teacher to translate (訳（やく）す) this letter.

Lesson ⑭

Indicating Intentions and Decisions

A

A middle-aged Japanese man starts a conversation with Claire, a young American student, who sits next to him on a bullet train bound for Osaka.

55

男の人　学生さんですね。どちらまで？

クレア　京都まで行きます。京都を見物するつもりです。

男の人　一人で？

クレア　いいえ。日本人の友達が京都にいますから、彼と
　　　　一緒に古いお寺や神社を見ようと思います。

男の人　そりゃあ結構ですね。で、いつまで京都に？

137

クレア　今、学校が休みだから10日ほどいることにしました。

男の人　奈良はどうですか。あの有名な大仏を見に。

クレア　見たいですが、今回は奈良へは行かないつもりです。

この次にします。

Man	You're a student, aren't you? Where are you headed?
Claire	I'm going to Kyoto. I plan to do some sightseeing there.
Man	All by yourself?
Claire	No. I have a Japanese friend in Kyoto, so I think I'll see some old temples and shrines with him.
Man	That's wonderful! So, how long do you intend to stay in Kyoto?
Claire	School is off right now, so I've decided to stay about ten days.
Man	How about (going to) Nara? To see that famous Big Buddha.
Claire	I want to see it, but I don't plan to go to Nara this time. I'll see it next time.

! Notes

1. 見物するつもりです "plan to do some sightseeing"

The pattern Vdic + つもりだ is used to express a firm intention. つもり is a pseudonoun—a noun that is never used independently and must be preceded by a modifier. It is usually followed by だ or です, but people tend to drop these copulas in casual conversation (see Note 2, p. 141).

2. 見ようと思います "I think I'll see"

The pattern Vvol + と思う is used to express thoughts about doing something. It is less decisive than the つもりだ pattern.

3. そりゃあ **"that"**
そりゃあ, or the shorter そりゃ, is a colloquial, informal form of それは and is used mainly by male speakers.

4. で **"so"**
で in this case is an abbreviated form of それで, which is used to change the topic.

5. いることにしました **"decided to stay"**
The pattern Vdic + ことにする expresses a decision to do something.

6. 行かないつもりです **"don't plan to go"**
The pattern Vneg + ないつもりだ expresses the speaker's intention not to do something.

7. この次にします **"will do it next time"**
The pattern N + にする expresses the speaker's choice from available alternatives.

B Yukari asks her friend Erika about her plans after graduation.

56

由香里（ゆかり） エリカ、学校（がっこう）を出（で）たら、どうするつもり？

エリカ ロサンゼルスの家（いえ）に帰（かえ）るつもりだったけど、当分（とうぶん）日本（にほん）で働（はたら）こうと思（おも）うの。

由香里　でも、フィアンセのピーターが待ってるんじゃない？

エリカ　彼が会社の仕事で日本へ来ることになったのよ。

由香里　へえ！　よかったわねえ。で、彼、どのくらい日
　　　　本にいるの？

エリカ　わからない。彼が日本で勤めている間、私は英語
　　　　を教えるか翻訳の仕事をしたいと思うの。

由香里　仕事は問題ないわよ。エリカは英語も日本語もで
　　　　きるから。

エリカ　そうだったらいいけど。

Yukari　Erika, what do you plan to do after graduating from school?

Erika　I'd intended to return to my home in Los Angeles, but I think I'll work in Japan for a while.

Yukari　But isn't your fiancé Peter waiting for you?

Erika　It's been decided that he'll come to Japan on company business.

Yukari　Really! How nice! So, how long will he be in Japan?

Erika　I don't know. While he's working in Japan, I think I'd like to either teach English or do translation work.

Yukari　No problem finding a job there. You can speak both English and Japanese.

Erika　I wish it were so (lit. It would be nice if that turns out to be the case).

⚠ Notes

1. 学校を出たら "after graduating from school"
The -たら form of a verb indicates that the action in the subordinate clause (the -たら clause) takes place before the action in the main clause. This form has several usages, but here it just means "after," as in "after graduating from school."

2. どうするつもり？ "What do you plan to do?"
This is the casual equivalent of どうするつもりですか.

3. 働こうと思うの "I think I'll work"
働こうと思う is the casual equivalent of 働こうと思います. The particle の at the end of the sentence—used by female speakers—softens the statement.

4. 来ることになった "It has been decided that he will come"
The pattern Vdic + ことになる is used to indicate a decision made by others, rather than by the speaker.

5. へえ！ "Really!"
へえ！expresses big surprise. Both male and female speakers use it.

6. 勤めている間 "while he is working"
The pattern Vte + いる間 is used to indicate a period during which an action is taking place.

7. そうだったら "if that is/turns out to be the case"
だったら, the -たら form of the copula だ, is equivalent to "if."

8. けど (sentence-final particle)
けど at the end of this sentence expresses Erika's uneasiness, her wish that what her friend is suggesting turns out to be true and her belief that it probably won't.

Agatha is studying Japanese flower arrangement. She wants to go to a flower exhibition being held at a culture center and asks her teacher to take her.

57

アガサ 先生はカルチャーセンターの生け花展示会にいらっしゃるおつもりですか。

先生 ええ、そのつもりです。アガサさんは？

アガサ 私も行こうと思っております。すみませんが、先生がいらっしゃる時、誘ってくださいませんか。

先生 ええ、いいですとも。いつにしましょうか。

アガサ 先生のご都合のいい日になさってください。

先生 じゃあ、あさっての午後にしましょう。あなたはいつもおけいこに熱心だこと。

アガサ 来月からお茶のおけいこも始めることにしました。お友達のお母さんがお茶の先生ですから。

先生 あなたは日本の伝統芸術に興味があるんですね。

アガサ ええ、とても。機会があれば尺八も習いたいと思っています。

先生 まあ、尺八も?!

Agatha　Sensei, do you intend to go to the flower-arrangement exhibition at the culture center?

Teacher　Yes, I do (lit. I have that intention). How about you, Agatha?

Agatha　I'm thinking of going, too. Sorry to bother you, but would you please take me with you when you go?

Teacher　Yes, of course. When shall we go?

Agatha　Please make it a day that is convenient for you.

Teacher　Then let's make it the day after tomorrow, in the afternoon. My, you are always so enthusiastic about your lessons.

Agatha　I've decided to start taking lessons in the tea ceremony next month. My friend's mother is a tea-ceremony instructor.

Teacher　You are really interested in traditional Japanese arts, aren't you?

Agatha　Yes, very much so. If I have the opportunity, I'd like to learn *shakuhachi* (the Japanese flute), too.

Teacher　Oh, my, *shakuhachi*, too?!

⚠ Notes

1. いらっしゃるおつもりですか **"Do you intend to go?"**
   This is the honorific equivalent of 行くつもりですか. The つもり is preceded by an honorific お-, and いらっしゃる is a special honorific verb meaning "to go."

2. 行こうと思っております **"I'm thinking of going"**
   This is the humble equivalent of 行こうと思っています.

3. 先生がいらっしゃる時 **"when you go"**
   時 (に) indicates the time when someone does something, something happens, or someone/something is in some state. 時

(when) is a pseudonoun used as a conjunction for the subordinate clause (the 時 clause).

4. いいですとも "of course"

The particle とも at the end of a sentence expresses the speaker's agreement with, or attunement to, what the other party has just said.

5. ご都合のいい日になさってください **"Please make it a day that is convenient for you"**

This is the N + にする pattern (Note 7, p.139) but with the honorific なさる used in the -てください form.

6. 熱心だこと **"enthusiastic"**

こと used at the end of a sentence in this pattern expresses the speaker's surprise or admiration. It is used chiefly by elderly women.

7. 機会があれば **"if I have the opportunity"**

あれば is a conditional form of ある and expresses a condition. The -たら form can also express a condition and be used in place of this -ば form, as in 機会があったら, for a more colloquial tone.

✏️ Practice

A. Express to the person indicated in parentheses your intention or decision to do the following.

1. You intend to return home before dinner. (your mother)

2. You intend not to go to college. (your teacher)

3. You have decided to buy a foreign car (外車^{がいしゃ}). (a friend)

4. You intend to climb (登^{のぼ}る) Mt. Fuji if you have the opportunity. (your boss)

5. You intend not to drive if it snows (雪^{ゆき}が降^ふる). (your boss)

B. Ask the person indicated in parentheses about his or her intention or plan to do the following.

1. Which will they decide on, coffee or tea (紅茶^{こうちゃ})? (a guest)

2. What will they do after graduating from college? (your younger brother)

3. Will they take their children on a trip? (your boss)

4. Will they do sightseeing in Kyoto with a Japanese friend? (your student)

5. Where will they work during summer vacation (夏休^{なつやす}み)? (a classmate)

Lesson 15

Asking Permission

A A patient recovering from an illness asks his doctor about what he is allowed to do.

患者 (かんじゃ)　先生、来週、旅行に出かけてもいいですか。

医者 (いしゃ)　いや、まだちょっと早いですね。せきが止まるまで待ちましょう。

患者 (かんじゃ)　この薬は続けて飲むんですか。

医者 (いしゃ)　熱が完全に下がれば飲まなくてもいいです。それまでは続けて飲まなければなりませんね。

患者　酒やタバコはどうですか。少しならかまいませんか。

医者　酒は少しぐらい飲んでもいいですが、タバコは絶
対に吸ってはいけませんよ。

Patient Doctor, may I go on a trip next week?

Doctor It's a little too soon, I'm afraid. Let's wait until you stop coughing.

Patient Do I continue to take this medicine?

Doctor If your fever goes down completely, you don't have to take it. Until then, you must continue taking it.

Patient How about drinking and smoking? Is it all right if it's just a little?

Doctor It's all right to drink a little liquor, but you should absolutely not smoke.

❗ Notes

1. 出かけてもいいですか "May I go?"
   The pattern Vte + もいいですか is used to request permission to do something. Vte + かまいませんか (Do you mind if I …?) may also be used to express the same idea.

2. 飲まなくてもいい "don't have to take it"
   The pattern Vneg + なくてもいい (です) is used to tell someone that he or she need not do something.

3. 飲まなければなりません "must take it"
   The pattern Vneg + なければならない / なければなりません is used to tell someone that he or she must do something. ならない / なりません can be interchanged with いけない / いけません.

4. 少しなら "**if it is a small amount**"

   少しなら (the pattern N + なら) expresses a condition. なら is the conditional form of the copula だ.

5. 吸ってはいけません "**should not smoke**"

   The pattern Vte + は + いけない / いけません is used to say that someone should not do something. いけない / いけません can be interchanged with だめだ / だめです.

B A middle school boy wants to use his older brother's bicycle and tries to persuade him to lend it to him.

59

弟　お兄ちゃん、お兄ちゃんの自転車、使っていい?

兄　だめだよ。もうすぐバイトに行かなきゃいけないんだ。

弟　貸してよ。登君の家へこの本、返しに行きたいから。

兄　歩いていけよ。遠くないんだろう?

弟　お願いだから貸してよ。じきに戻るから。今、持っていくって約束したんだもの。

兄　しょうがないなあ。すぐ帰らなくちゃだめだぞ。バイトに遅れたらクビになるんだぞ。あの店のマネージャー、時間にうるさいんだから。

弟　わかってる。サンキュー。

Younger Brother	Brother, can I use your bike?
Older Brother	Nope. I have to go to work pretty soon.
Younger Brother	Lend it to me. I want to go to Noboru's house to return this book.
Older Brother	So walk. It's not far, is it?
Younger Brother	Please, please lend it to me! I'll be back in no time. I promised him I'd bring it back to him now.
Older Brother	I guess I have no choice, then. But you have to come back right away. If I'm late for work, I'll get fired. The manager at that store is strict about time.
Younger Brother	I understand. Thank you.

⚠ Notes

1. 使っていい？ "Can I use …?"
   This is the casual equivalent of 使ってもいいですか. The も is omitted in fast speech.

2. バイト "side job"
   バイト is a shortening of アルバイト (see Note 1, p. 130).

3. 行かなきゃいけない "have to go"
   行かなきゃいけない is a contraction of 行かなければならない and is used in informal speech.

4. お願いだから "please, please," "I'm pleading with you"
   お願いだから is used to make a desperate plea.

5. 持っていくって "I said I'd bring it"
   持っていくって is the casual form of 持っていくと. The ending って is a colloquial quotation marker used in place of the quotation particle と.

6. しょうがない "It can't be helped," "There is little choice"

しょうがない is a contraction of 仕様 / 仕方がない (lit. There is no way) and conveys the idea that there is nothing for it (but to give in).

7. 帰らなくちゃ "must return"

帰らなくちゃ is a contraction of 帰らなくては and is used in fast, informal speech. Vneg + なくて + は + だめだ is the affirmative form of the pattern Vte + は + だめだ mentioned on p. 148 (Note 5) as a variation of Vte + は + いけない.

8. クビになる "get fired"

This is an idiomatic expression meaning "to get fired."

C A secretary is about to go to the post office to send a package and asks her boss, the company president, if he needs anything while she is out.

60

秘書　社長、今から郵便局へこの小包を出しに<u>行っても</u>

<u>よろしいでしょうか</u>。

社長　ああ、頼むよ。

秘書　書留で<u>送らなくてもよろしゅうございますか</u>。

社長　そうだなあ。普通でいいだろう。

秘書　郵便局の帰りにデパートへ<u>寄ってまいりますが</u>、

何かご必要な物はございませんか。

社長 いや、今のところ別に。

秘書 来週の息子さんのお誕生日にバースデーケーキを
ご注文なさらなければなりませんね。

社長 そうだな。ついでに注文してきてもらえるかな。

秘書 かしこまりました。

Secretary President, may I go to the post office to mail this package now?

President Yes, thanks (lit. I will ask you to do so).

Secretary Is it all right if I don't send it by registered mail?

President Hmm. Ordinary mail would be fine, I suppose.

Secretary I'm going to stop by the department store on my way back from the post office. Is there anything you need?

President No, nothing in particular at the moment.

Secretary You need to order a birthday cake for your son's birthday next week, don't you?

President That's right. Could you please order it for me while you're there?

Secretary Certainly.

❗ Notes

1. 行ってもよろしいでしょうか "May I go?"
   行ってもよろしいでしょうか is the superpolite form of 行って

もいいですか and is used for asking a superior for permission to do something.

2. 送らなくてもよろしゅうございますか "**Is it all right if I don't send it?**"
送らなくてもよろしゅうございますか is the superpolite form of 送らなくてもいいですか and is interchangeable with 送らなくてもよろしいでしょうか. The polite adjective よろしい changes to よろしゅう before ございます.

3. 寄ってまいります "**(go/come and) stop by**"
This is the humble form of the compound verb 寄っていく / 寄ってくる (go/come and stop by), where いく / くる indicates the direction in which the action proceeds (see Note 4, p. 117). まいる is a humble form of 行く / 来る.

4. ご注文なさらなければなりません "**You need to order …**"
ご注文なさらなければなりません is the superpolite equivalent of 注文しなければならない.

5. ついでに "**while you are there,**" "**at the same time**"
ついでに is an adverb that indicates a person's taking advantage of a situation to do something additional.

Practice

What would you say in the following situations?

1. You (a secretary) want to ask the company president if it is all right to open (開ける) a package.

2. You want to tell your student that he should not write (書く) in pencil (えんぴつ).

3. You want to ask your mother if it is all right to go camping (キャンプ) with your friend Tom.

4. You want to tell your teacher that you have to return a book to the library by Wednesday (水曜日).

5. You want to ask your older sister if it is all right to borrow (借りる) her necklace (ネックレス).

6. You want to ask the manager if it is all right not to come to work tomorrow.

7. You want to tell your boy that he should not leave (置く) his bicycle in the yard (庭).

8. You want to tell a customer that he doesn't have to pay (支払う) the fee (料金) now.

Lesson 16

Relating Personal Experience

A

Mr. Sakamoto asks Mr. Benson, who is temporarily working in the Tokyo office of their company, about how he spends his free time.

61

坂本　ベンソンさん、日本の映画は好きですか。

ベンソン　はい。時々、友達と見ることがあります。侍映画は言葉がわからなくても面白いですよ。

坂本　歌舞伎を見ましたか。

ベンソン　歌舞伎は一度見たことがあります。役者の衣装も舞台も、とても豪華でした。

154

坂本　楽^{たの}しかったですか。

ベンソン　日本語^{にほんご}が全然^{ぜんぜん}わかりませんでした。この次^{つぎ}は、イヤホンで英語^{えいご}の説明^{せつめい}を聞^ききながら見るつもりです。

坂本　文楽^{ぶんらく}は？

ベンソン　文楽はまだ見たことはありません。いつか見たいと思^{おも}っています。

坂本　相撲^{すもう}も面白いですよ。

ベンソン　テレビでしか見たことがありません。国技館^{こくぎかん}で見たら、もっとエキサイトするでしょうね。

Sakamoto	Mr. Benson, do you like Japanese movies?
Benson	Yes. I sometimes watch them with friends. Samurai films are interesting, even if I don't understand the language.
Sakamoto	Have you seen Kabuki?
Benson	I've seen Kabuki once. The actors' costumes and the stage were all very gorgeous.
Sakamoto	Did you enjoy it?
Benson	I didn't understand the Japanese. Next time I plan to see it while listening on earphones to the English commentary.
Sakamoto	How about Bunraku?
Benson	I haven't seen Bunraku yet. I'd like to see it someday.
Sakamoto	Sumo, too, is interesting.
Benson	I've only seen it on TV. It would be more exciting to see it at the Kokugikan.

⚠️ Notes

1. 時々見ることがあります lit. "There are times when I see …"
   The pattern Vdic +ことがある is used to say that one does something from time to time. The adverbs 時々 (sometimes), よく (often), and たまに (occasionally) sometimes modify this pattern, giving a clearer indication of the frequency.

2. 言葉がわからなくても "even if I don't understand the language"
   The pattern Vneg + なくても expresses a negative condition.

3. 見たことがあります "have seen …"
   The pattern Vta + ことがある is used to say that one has done something in the past or has had a certain experience.

4. 見たことはありません "have not seen …"
   見たことはない is a negative form of 見たことがある, where は marks 見たこと (the act of seeing) as a contrastive element. The idea is that Mr. Benson has not seen Bunraku, but has perhaps heard of it or read about it.

5. テレビでしか "only on TV"
   The particle で after a noun indicates a means to do something, and the particle しか followed by a negative means "only."

6. 見たことがありません "I have not seen it"
   見たことがない (with が used instead of は) is the standard negative form of 見たことがある and implies no contrast.

B Two young wives, Naomi and Ayako, talk about their husbands and about their mutual friend Sachiko.

62

直美 お宅のご主人、週末は何していらっしゃるの？

綾子 そうねえ、ゴルフに行くこともあるし、家でごろごろしていることもあるわ。

直美 うちの主人はスポーツに興味がないから、ゴルフに行くことはないの。

綾子 それはそうと、この頃幸子さんに会うことある？

直美 めったにないわ。彼女、あれやこれやで忙しいんでしょう。

綾子 あのね、私、銀座のレストランで、彼女のボーイフレンドを見たことあるのよ。話さなかったけど。

直美 ふーん。だれかと一緒だったの？

綾子 うん。若い、きれいな人。これ内緒よ。

Naomi   What does your husband do (lit. What is your husband in the habit of doing) on weekends?

Ayako   Well, sometimes he goes golfing and sometimes he loafs about the house.

Naomi   My husband has no interest in sports, so he never goes golfing.

Ayako   By the way, do you ever see Sachiko these days?

Naomi   Hardly ever. She's probably busy with this and that.

Ayako   Guess what! I once saw her boyfriend in a restaurant in Ginza. I didn't speak to him, though.

Naomi   I see. Was he with someone?

Ayako   Yes. A young, pretty woman. It's a secret, okay?

⚠ Notes

1. 何していらっしゃるの？ **"What is he doing?"**
The pattern Vte + いらっしゃる is the honorific form of Vte + いる. Here it expresses the repetition of an action. Naomi uses the honorific form because she is talking about the actions of Ayako's husband.

2. ごろごろしている **"loafing about"**
ごろごろする is an idiomatic expression meaning literally "to do nothing but roll around."

3. それはそうと **"by the way"**
This phrase is used to change the subject.

4. あのね **"Look!" "Say!"**
あのね is used to get someone's attention, to get her to focus on what one is about to say, in a casual, friendly conversation.

5. 見たことある **"have seen …"**
This is a casual form. Note that Ayako has dropped が because this is a casual conversation and が is just a little cumbersome.

6. 若い、きれいな人 "young, pretty person"

Ayako could have said 若くて、きれいな人, but she is speaking what comes to mind as she remembers the scene, without caring about the details of grammar.

C

Mrs. Seki talks with Mr. White, a young assistant to her husband, with the intention of inviting him to a tea party at her home.

63

関　ホワイトさん、野口博士にお会いになったことある？

ホワイト　いいえ、まだお目にかかったことはございません。先生のお話はテレビでお聞きしたことがありますが。

関　明日のうちのティーパーティーに、野口先生をお招きしてるのよ。よかったら、あなたもいらっしゃらない？

ホワイト　はい。先生にお目にかかれたら光栄です。必ずおうかがいいたします。

関　先生は最近アフリカからお帰りになったところだから、きっと面白い冒険談がうかがえますよ。

ホワイト　素晴らしいですね。楽しみにしております。

Seki	Mr. White, have you met Dr. Noguchi?
White	No, I have not met him yet. I have heard his talks on TV, though.
Seki	I've invited Dr. Noguchi to a tea party at our house tomorrow. Would you, too, like to come?
White	Yes. It would be an honor to meet him. I'll definitely come.
Seki	He has just come back from Africa, so I'm sure we can hear about his interesting adventures.
White	Splendid. I am looking forward to it.

⚠ Notes

1. お会いになったことある？ **"Have you met …?"**
   Mrs. Seki uses お会いになった, the honorific form of 会った (met), with the plain-style ある (not the polite あります) to make her words sound elegant yet friendly.

2. お目にかかったことはございません **"I have not met …"**
   This is the superpolite equivalent of 会ったことはない. お目にかかる is a special honorific verb meaning "to meet."

3. おうかがいいたします **"I will come"**
   うかがう is a special humble verb meaning "to come" or "to go." It is made even more humble by going through the お + Vstem + いたす pattern.

4. お帰りになったところだ **"has just returned"**
   The pattern Vta + ところだ expresses an action that has just been completed.

5. うかがえます **"can hear"**
   This is the polite-style potential form of the special humble verb うかがう (hear).

🖉 Practice

How would you express the following to the person in parentheses?

1. You have taught English at a high school (高校) in Tokyo.

(your boss)

2. You (a female) lived in Germany (ドイツ) when you were a child. (a classmate)

3. You (a male) have never eaten raw fish (さしみ).   (a coworker)

4. You (a female) hardly ever go out for dinner (夕食) alone (一人で). (your sister)

5. Your husband sometimes drinks at a bar with his friends.

(a neighbor)

6. You have never been to Dr. Hara's (原博士) house.

(your teacher)

7. You have seen sumo only on TV. (your teacher)

8. You (a male) sometimes speak with your Japanese friends in Japanese. (a classmate)

Conjecturing

A A Japanese class is going to take a field trip to a sake factory. Before the trip, the teacher sounds out his class to figure out how many students are going to go.

64

先生 来週の酒造工場の見学に行かない人はいますか。

リタ サラさんは多分行かないでしょう。お母さんが病気だそうです。

ビル 僕も行けないかもしれません。試合でくじいた足首がまだ痛むので。

先生 ディックさんは？ だれか知っていますか。

ジョン　ディックは<u>行くにちがいない</u>です。ゆうべ電話で話しました。彼の友達も<u>行くはず</u>です。風邪が治ったので、明日、学校に<u>来るよう</u>です。

先生　それはよかったですね。ほかにだれか行けない人がいたら、今日中に知らせてください。

Teacher Is there anyone who is not going to go on next week's field trip to the sake factory?

Rita Sara probably won't go. I hear that her mother is ill.

Bill I might not be able to go either. My ankle, which I sprained in a tournament, still hurts.

Teacher How about Dick? Does anyone know?

John Dick will go, no doubt. I talked with him on the phone last night. I expect his friend will go too. He got over his cold, so it seems he will come (back) to school tomorrow.

Teacher I'm glad to hear that. If there is anyone else who cannot go, please let me know today.

⚠ Notes

1. 行かない人 "person who will not go"
In the pattern Vneg + ない + N, the negative form of the verb modifies the following noun.

2. 行かないでしょう "probably won't go"
The pattern Vneg + ないでしょう / ないだろう expresses a negative conjecture. For a positive conjecture, the dictionary form +

でしょう / だろう is used: 行くでしょう / 行くだろう.

3. 病気だそうです **"I hear that she is ill"**
The pattern S + そうです / そうだ expresses hearsay—information the speaker heard or obtained indirectly.

4. 行けないかもしれません **"might not be able to go"**
The pattern Vneg + ないかもしれません / ないかもしれない expresses the speaker's speculation that someone will not do something or that something will not happen.

5. くじいた足首 **"the ankle that I sprained"**
In the Vta + N pattern, the -た form of the verb modifies the following noun.

6. 行くにちがいない **"No doubt he will go"**
The pattern Vdic + にちがいない / にちがいありません expresses a confident guess that someone will do something or that something will happen.

7. 行くはずです **"I expect he will go"**
The pattern Vdic + はずです / はずだ expresses an expectation that someone will do something, or that something will happen, as a natural outcome.

8. 来るようです **"It seems that he will come"**
The pattern Vdic +ようです / ようだ expresses an impression or a conjecture based on firsthand information.

B Fumiko and Noriko, young employees in the company, gossip about Ms. Hayashi, their senior by about ten years.

65

文子　林さんが会社を辞めること知ってる？

典子　え！　あの人が今、仕事を辞めるはずがないわ。課長のポストをねらっているんだもの。

文子　結婚するらしいわよ。

典子　へえ！　で、相手はだれ？　私達の知ってる人？

文子　あなた、会ったことあるかもしれないわ。うちの関連会社の国際部の部長でアメリカ人だって。

典子　覚えていないわ。でも、ずいぶん急な話ね。

文子　秘密でデートしてたにちがいないわ。その人が急にアメリカの本社に戻ることになったみたいよ。

Fumiko Did you know that Ms. Hayashi is leaving the company?

Noriko What? There's no way she'd quit her job now. She's aiming to become (lit. for the post of) section chief.

Fumiko It seems she's getting married.

Noriko Really? And who is the man (lit. the partner)? Someone we know?

Fumiko You might have met him. I hear he is the head of the international department of our affiliated company, and an American.

Noriko   I don't remember (meeting him). But what a sudden turn of events, isn't it?

Fumiko   No doubt she has been dating him in secret. It seems to have been decided suddenly that he will return to the head office in America.

⚠ Notes

1. 会社を辞めること "**that she is leaving the company**"
The nominalizer こと in this case turns the clause coming before it into a noun phrase, which then serves as the direct object of the verb 知っている (though を is dropped).

2. 辞めるはずがない "**There's no way she would quit**"
The pattern Vdic + はずがない expresses a strong negative assertion.

3. 結婚するらしい "**It seems she is getting married**"
The pattern Vdic + らしい expresses conjecture based on reliable information—what one has heard, read, or observed.

4. 私達の知ってる人 "**someone we know**"
In a modifying clause (relative clause), the subject marker が may change to the particle の: 私達が → 私達の.

5. 会ったことあるかもしれない "**might have met**"
This is a casual equivalent of 会ったことがあるかもしれません.

6. アメリカ人だって "**I hear that he is an American**"
This is a casual equivalent of アメリカ人だそうです.

7. デートしてたにちがいない "No doubt she has been dating"
This is a casual equivalent of デートしていたにちがいありません.

8. 戻ることになったみたい "It seems to have been decided that he will return"
This is a casual equivalent of 戻ることになったようです.

C

Mr. Morita, who is going to the airport to meet Mr. Morris, a buyer from New York City, talks about Mr. Morris's arrival with the company president and his secretary.

66

森田　ニューヨークのバイヤーのモリスさんが空港にお着きになるのは何時ですか。

社長　４時のはずだが飛行機が遅れるかもしれないな。

秘書　空港にはどなたがお出迎えにいらっしゃるのですか。

森田　岡崎部長とご一緒に私がまいります。

秘書　空港からまっすぐホテルへいらっしゃるんですか。

森田　ええ。長いフライトでお疲れにちがいないから、いったんホテルにお連れいたします。

社長　空港への道は、今あちこち工事中で、車の渋滞がひどいそうだ。

森田 そうらしいですね。<u>遅れ(おく)ないように早(はや)めに出(で)かけ

るつもりです</u>。

| Morita | What time is Mr. Morris, the buyer from New York, arriving at the airport? |

Morita   What time is Mr. Morris, the buyer from New York, arriving at the airport?

President   He is expected to arrive at four o'clock, but the plane might be delayed.

Secretary   Who is going to the airport to meet him?

Morita   I'm going with General Manager Okazaki.

Secretary   Are you going straight to the hotel from the airport?

Morita   Yes. (Mr. Morris) will no doubt be exhausted from the long flight, so we will take him to the hotel as the first order of business.

President   I hear the road to the airport is under construction here and there, and the traffic jams are terrible.

Morita   It seems so. We plan to leave early so as not to be late.

⚠ Notes

1. お着きになるの "the time when he will arrive"
The particle の following お着きになる, the honorific form of the verb 着く (arrive), is used as a pronoun for "time" and is modified by お着きになる.

2. 4時のはずだ "is expected at four o'clock"
The pseudonoun はず is modified by the phrase 4時の.

3. お出迎えにいらっしゃる "go to meet"
お出迎えにいらっしゃる is the honorific equivalent of 出迎えにいく. 出迎え is the -ます stem of 出迎える (meet, welcome).

4. まいります **"go"**

This is a special humble verb meaning "to go" or "to come."

5. お疲れにちがいないから **"because he must be tired"**

In the subordinate clause (the から clause), the plain form ち
がいない may be used instead of the polite ちがいありません
since the speech style is determined by the verb in the main
clause. お疲れ is the noun form of the verb 疲れる (get tired),
with the honorific prefix お- attached.

6. お連れいたします **"will take him"**

This is a humble equivalent of 連れていく / 連れていきます
(take [a person somewhere]). See also Sentence 6, p. 26.

7. 遅れないように **"so as not to be late"**

The pattern Vneg + ないように expresses a reason or motive for
an action.

Practice

Complete the following sentences.

1. 息子の孝が入院したの。私、あなたと一緒に旅行に＿＿＿＿＿＿

＿＿＿＿＿＿＿。

My son Takashi has been hospitalized. I might not be able to go on the trip with you.

2. 「この人だかりは何ですか」
「この交差点で交通事故が＿＿＿＿＿＿＿＿＿＿＿」

"What is this crowd all about?"
"It seems there was a traffic accident at this intersection."

3. 今晩の宴会は社長が出席＿＿＿＿＿＿＿＿＿＿＿。

The company president is expected to attend tonight's banquet.

4. サムが学期の途中で学校を＿＿＿＿＿＿＿＿＿＿。

I can't believe Sam is quitting school in the middle of the term.

5. 「次の課長はだれ＿＿＿＿＿＿＿＿＿＿＿」
「小泉＿＿＿＿＿＿＿＿＿＿。彼、部長の甥だから」

"Who might the next section chief be?"
"Koizumi, no doubt. He's the general manager's nephew."

6. ブラウン先生は日本の宗教についてご本を＿＿＿＿＿＿＿＿。

I hear that Professor Brown is writing a book on Japanese religion.

7. 天気予報によると、明日は雨＿＿＿＿＿＿＿＿わよ。ゴルフは

できない＿＿＿＿＿＿＿。

According to the weather forecast, it seems it will rain tomorrow. We probably can't play golf.

Lesson 18

Describing the Actions of Giving and Receiving

A Mr. Suzuki and Mr. Hill, who belong to the same photography club, talk about their respective experience.

鈴木　ヒルさん、いいカメラを持っていますね。

ヒル　日本人の友達にもらいました。彼に時々英語を教

　　　えてあげるので、お礼にこれをくれたのです。

鈴木　そうなんですか。ヒルさんはどんな写真が得意で

　　　すか。

ヒル　私はまだ初心者ですから……。撮った写真をみん

なに見てもらいたいです。鈴木さんはもうプロに近いんでしょう?

鈴木 いや、なかなか。まだアマですよ。私は自然を撮るのが好きで、日の出や日の入りの写真を何枚も撮りましたよ。

ヒル いつか見せていただきたいですね。

Suzuki Mr. Hill, what a fine camera you have!

Hill I got it from a Japanese friend. I teach him English sometimes, so he gave this to me as a gift.

Suzuki Really? What kind of photos are you good at taking?

Hill I'm still a beginner.... I want to have people see the photos I've taken. Mr. Suzuki, I suppose you are already close to being a professional.

Suzuki No, not so easily. I'm still an amateur. I like to take pictures of nature and have taken many photos of sunrises and sunsets.

Hill I'd enjoy seeing them someday.

! Notes

1. 友達にもらいました "I got it from a friend"

The pattern N (person) + に / から + もらう indicates that the speaker (or someone with whom he can empathize) receives something from someone whose social status is about equal to or lower than his own.

2. 教えてあげる "I teach him"

The pattern Vte + あげる expresses a person's doing a favorable action for someone whose status is about equal to his own.

3. これをくれた "gave this to me"

The verb くれる (give) is used when a person receives something from someone whose status is about equal to or lower than his own.

4. 見てもらいたい "I want to have people see …"

The pattern Vte + もらいたい indicates a person's desire to receive a favorable action from someone whose status is about equal to or lower than his own.

5. 見せていただきたい "I want to have you show them to me"

The pattern Vte + いただきたい indicates a person's desire to receive a favorable action from someone whose status is higher than his own. In this case, however, the speaker uses it just to be polite.

B **A daughter who is in high school talks with her mother about the bird her younger brother has brought home.**

68

娘　まあ、かわいい小鳥ねえ。どうしたの？

母　昇が学校の友達からもらってきたのよ。

娘　へえ！　お母さん、餌やった？

母　さっき昇がやってたわ。あの子、今友達の家へ鳥

の本を貸してもらいに行ってるの。鳥の世話は自分でするそうよ。

娘　初めはやるけど、あとでお母さんに世話してもらうんじゃない?

母　あなたもたまには手伝ってやりなさい。

娘　いやよ。受験準備で忙しいんだから。今から図書館へ行ってくるわ。

母　行く途中でこの手紙、ポストに入れてくれない?

娘　オーケー。

Daughter	Oh, what a cute bird! Where did it come from?
Mother	Noboru got it from a friend at school.
Daughter	Really! Mother, did you feed it?
Mother	Noboru was feeding it a while ago. He has gone to his friend's house to borrow (lit. to have his friend lend him) a book on birds. He said he'll take care of the bird by himself.
Daughter	He will in the beginning, but later he'll have you take care of it, no?
Mother	You, too, will help him once in a while.
Daughter	No way. I'm busy preparing for the entrance exams. I'm going to the library now.
Mother	On your way, would you drop this letter in the mailbox for me?
Daughter	Okay.

⚠ Notes

1. 餌やった？ "**Did you feed it?**"

The verb やる (give) is used in situations where the recipient is a child, animal, or plant.

2. あの子 "**he/she**"

あの子 is a pronoun used to refer to children and young women.

3. 貸してもらいに "**to have him lend**"

The phrase 貸してもらいに (with a motion verb) indicates the purpose of an action when a person moves from one place to another. 貸してもらいに and 借りに (to borrow) basically mean the same thing, differing only in that the former implies a favor someone is asking for while the latter does not.

4. 世話してもらうんじゃない？ "**Isn't it that he will have you take care of it?**"

世話してもらうんじゃない？ is a casual equivalent of 世話してもらうのではありませんか, where の is turning the phrase before it into a noun phrase.

5. 手伝ってやりなさい "**Help him**"

The pattern Vte + やりなさい expresses a command to do something as a favor for a child and is usually used by parents when speaking to their children.

6. 入れてくれない？ "**Would you mind putting (this) in (the mailbox)?**"

The pattern Vte + くれる expresses a person's doing, of her own volition, a favorable action for the speaker (or someone with whom the speaker can empathize). The form -てくれない？ or -てくれませんか (polite) is used when the speaker is asking for a favor. And when the asked-for favor is done, the speaker may describe the action with the pattern Vte +もらった / もらいました.

Mrs. Koga meets Ms. Abe on the way to church, where they are expected to help set up a fundraising event.

69

古賀　きれいなスカーフですね！　その藤色のジャケットにぴったり。

安部　秋山さんのお姉さんからいただいたんです。パリで買ってきてくださったのよ。

古賀　その方は確かピアノの先生でいらっしゃいますね。

安部　ええ。いとこの子供がピアノを教えていただいています。

古賀　あら、向こうに立っていらっしゃるのは、秋山さんとリードさんじゃありませんか。

安部　そうですね。教会員じゃないのに、リードさんは教会の行事でいつも私達を手伝ってくださいますね。

古賀　ありがたいわ。クリスマスに何かプレゼントをさ

し上げるかディナーに招待してさし上げるかした

らどうでしょう？

安部　ええ。皆さんもきっと賛成なさると思うわ。

Koga	What a beautiful scarf! A perfect match with that lilac jacket.
Abe	I got it from Ms. Akiyama's older sister. She bought it for me in Paris.
Koga	She's a piano teacher, isn't she?
Abe	Yes. My cousin's child is getting piano lessons from her.
Koga	Oh, aren't those two standing over there Ms. Akiyama and Mrs. Reed?
Abe	Yes, they are. Though not a church member herself, Mrs. Reed always helps us with (preparations for) church events.
Koga	We are very grateful. Come Christmas, how about we give her a present or invite her to dinner?
Abe	Good. I'm sure that everybody will agree.

⚠ Notes

1. いただいたんです **"I got/received"**
   いただく is a special humble verb used when the receiver gets something from someone whose status is higher than her own. Here Ms. Abe uses it in the past tense followed by the polite ん です because she is explaining the circumstances surrounding a scarf she was given and which Mrs. Koga has commented on.

2. 買ってきてくださった **"she bought it for me"**
   The pattern Vte + くださる is used when the status of the performer of a favorable action is higher than that of the receiver.

3. 確か "if memory serves me"

確か is an adverb that expresses the speaker's conjecture based on memory: "if memory serves me," "if I recall correctly," etc.

4. 教えていただいています "is getting lessons"

The pattern Vte + いただく is used when a favorable action comes from someone whose status is higher than that of the receiver. The difference between Vte + いただく and Vte + くださる is as follows: in the former, いただく is a verb that describes the action of receiving, and the subject of the sentence is the speaker or someone with whom she can empathize. In the latter, the action described by くださる is one of giving, and the sentence's subject is the person who does the beneficial action.

5. いつも手伝ってくださいます "always helps us"

This is the Vte + くださる pattern from Note 2, here used in the present tense together with いつも to indicate a habitual action.

6. さし上げる "give"

さし上げる is a special humble verb used when the giver gives something to someone whose status is higher than her own.

7. 招待してさし上げる "invite"

The idea of someone humbly doing something for another's benefit is expressed by Vte + さし上げる. In this pattern, the recipient of the favorable action is someone whose social status is higher than that of the doer of the action. Because it can sound presumptuous, it is best to avoid using this pattern when speaking directly to a superior about doing something for him, especially if the action is something he can't do himself. In such cases, it is better to use a humble verb that does not imply a favor.

Practice

Circle the correct word from among the options in parentheses.

1. 良子、花に水（あげた / やった / くれた）？
   Yoshiko, did you water the flowers?

2. 長谷川先生に推薦状を書いて（もらい / さし上げ / いただき）ました。
   I had Professor Hasegawa write a letter of recommendation for me.

3. 僕がサムに日本語を教えて（やって / あげて / いただいて）、サムが僕に英語を教えて（くれる / あげる / やる）んです。
   I teach Japanese to Sam, and Sam teaches English to me.

4. 私は課長に京都のお土産を（もらい / あげ / さし上げ）ます。
   I will give the section chief a souvenir from Kyoto.

5. 高木先生からこの辞書を（いただき / ください / もらい）ました。
   I got this dictionary from Professor Takagi.

6. 娘にコンサートのチケットを買って（やり / もらい / いただき）ます。
   I will have my daughter buy me the concert tickets.

7. 小池さんのお父様がローマでお撮りになった写真を見せて（くれ / ください / さし上げ）ました。
   Mr. Koike's father showed me pictures he had taken in Rome.

8. 兄は時々、子供達を動物園へ連れていって（あげ / やり / もらい）ます。
   My older brother sometimes takes his children to the zoo.

Lesson 19

Using Passive, Causative, and Causative-Passive Forms

A Mr. Sonoda and Mr. Kotani happen to meet in the train and talk about the security in their neighborhood.

70

園田 昨日の事件の犯人は警察に逮捕されましたか。

小谷 いや、まだのようです。最近この辺りも物騒になりましたね。

園田 そうですね。若い女性が変な男に追いかけられたり、駅前の駐輪場に置いておいた自転車やスクーターを盗まれたり。

小谷　うちでは息子に、電車に乗る時、駅まで自転車で
　　　行くのを止めさせました。

園田　歩いたほうが健康にいいですよ。そんなに遠くな
　　　いんですから。

小谷　息子は親には歩かされるし、部活では走らされる
　　　し、身がもたないって、こぼしていますよ。

Sonoda　Was the criminal in yesterday's incident arrested by the police?

Kotani　No, it doesn't seem so. Recently this area also has become unsafe, hasn't it?

Sonoda　That's right. What with a young woman being chased by a strange man, and people having their bikes and scooters stolen from where they had left them at the bicycle lot in front of the station.

Kotani　We made our son stop going to the station by bike when he takes the train.

Sonoda　Walking is better for his health. It's not that far (to the station).

Kotani　Our son is grumbling, saying that he is made to walk by his parents and made to run in his club activities (at school), and that he is overexerting himself.

⚠️ Notes

1. 警察に逮捕されました "**was arrested by the police**"

The pattern Vneg + れる / られる expresses the passive form, in which something is done to the subject of the sentence. れる is attached to regular I verbs and られる to regular II verbs (see Appendix B). The irregular verbs 来る and する become 来られる and される. So 逮捕する (arrest) in this case becomes 逮捕される (be arrested). The agent, or performer of the action (in this case, the police), takes the particle に. There are two types of passive sentence in Japanese: the direct passive and the indirect passive. The sentence here is a direct passive and is similar to the English passive in that the object of the active sentence becomes the subject of the passive one.

2. 駐輪場に置いておいた自転車 "**bikes left in the bicycle lot**"

The pattern Vte + おく expresses an action performed in advance for a future convenience. The noun 自転車 is modified by the preceding clause. The idea is that the bikes were not just put in the lot, but left there to be picked up later and ridden home.

3. スクーターを盗まれ "**having their scooters stolen**"

The passive sentence (人が) スクーターを盗まれた is an example of the indirect passive. The indirect passive is different from the direct passive and the English passive in that the direct object of the active sentence remains as the direct object and the person who becomes the subject of the passive sentence is the one who is adversely affected by someone else's action or by an unpleasant event. For this passive, both transitive and intransitive verbs may be used. (See Notes 1 and 3 on pp. 187-88 for examples of intransitive verbs in the passive form.)

4. たり **(ellipsis)**

In both spoken and written Japanese, する in the Vtari … Vtari + する pattern is sometimes omitted. This is another example of ellipsis; the speaker uses the minimum number of words to get his point across.

5. 止めさせました **"made him stop …"**

The pattern Vneg + せる / させる expresses the causative form, in which the subject of the sentence makes someone (marked by the particle に) do something. せる is attached to regular I verbs and させる to regular II verbs (see Appendix B). 来る and する become 来させる and させる. There is also a shortened form of the causative form in which す is used instead of せる for regular I verbs, and さす is used instead of させる for regular II verbs: 止める (dictionary form) → 止めさせる (causative form) → 止めさす (shortened causative form).

6. 歩かされる **"is made to walk"**

This is a shortened form of the causative-passive form ordinarily expressed by the pattern Vneg + せられる / させられる, where せられる is attached to regular I verbs and させられる to regular II verbs, and where the irregular verbs する and 来る become させられる and 来させられる, respectively (see Appendix B). In this shortened causative-passive form, which only exists for regular I verbs, れる is added to the negative stem of the verb's shortened causative form as follows: 歩く (dictionary form) → 歩かす (causative form) → 歩かさ (negative stem of the causative form) → 歩かされる (shortened causative-passive form). In the causative-passive form, the subject of the sentence is made to do something.

7. 身<ruby>み</ruby>がもたない lit. "(his) health will not hold out"

身<ruby>み</ruby>がもたない is an idiom meaning to overexert oneself to the point where one's health is compromised—to ruin one's health.

B Beth comes to Reiko's office to invite her out to lunch. They gossip about their coworker Yoriko.

71

ベス　玲子<ruby>れいこ</ruby>さん、お昼<ruby>ひる</ruby>、食<ruby>た</ruby>べに行<ruby>い</ruby>かない?

玲子<ruby>れいこ</ruby>　ちょっと待<ruby>ま</ruby>って、これ書<ruby>か</ruby>いてしまうまで。係長<ruby>かかりちょう</ruby>を待<ruby>ま</ruby>たせてるから。

ベス　頼子<ruby>よりこ</ruby>さんも誘<ruby>さそ</ruby>う? 彼女<ruby>かのじょ</ruby>この頃<ruby>ごろ</ruby>なんだか寂<ruby>さび/さみ</ruby>しそうだわ。

玲子<ruby>れいこ</ruby>　彼女<ruby>かのじょ</ruby>、先週<ruby>せんしゅう</ruby>ボスが変<ruby>か</ruby>わって、きつい仕事<ruby>しごと</ruby>を手伝<ruby>てつだ</ruby>わされるし、彼氏<ruby>かれし</ruby>には振<ruby>ふ</ruby>られるし、踏<ruby>ふ</ruby>んだり蹴<ruby>け</ruby>ったりだって言<ruby>い</ruby>ってたわ。

ベス　かわいそうに。ちょっと彼女<ruby>かのじょ</ruby>のところに寄<ruby>よ</ruby>ってみようか。ところで、それ、素敵<ruby>すてき</ruby>なバッグね!

玲子<ruby>れいこ</ruby>　友達<ruby>ともだち</ruby>に高<ruby>たか</ruby>い物<ruby>もの</ruby>、買<ruby>か</ruby>わされちゃったの。

Beth	Reiko, want to go out for lunch?
Reiko	Wait a minute—until I finish writing this. I'm making the subsection chief wait (to get this).
Beth	Should we invite Yoriko, too? She somehow looks lonely these days.
Reiko	She got a new boss last week (lit. last week her boss changed) and she's being made to do hard work—and worse, she was dumped by her boyfriend. This is adding insult to injury (lit. being trod on and kicked), she says.
Beth	Poor thing. Let's stop by her desk. By the way, that is a gorgeous bag!
Reiko	My friend talked me into buying an expensive thing (lit. I was made to buy an expensive thing by my friend).

! Notes

1. 書いてしまう "finish writing"

The pattern Vte + しまう expresses with emphasis the completion of an action, sometimes with regret. In this case, 書いてしまう simply means "finish writing" and expresses no regret.

2. 待たせてる "am making (him) wait"

This is a casual equivalent of 待たせている (the causative form of 待つ in the -ている form to indicate a current state resulting from an action).

3. 寂しそうだ "looks lonely"

The pattern Adj stem + そうだ expresses the speaker's judgment based on what she sees or hears.

4. 手伝わされる "is made to help …"

手伝わされる is the shortened version of the causative-passive form 手伝わせられる and is made by attaching れる to the

negative stem of the shortened causative verb 手伝わす: 手伝わ
さ (negative stem) → 手伝わされる (shortened causative-passive
form). 手伝わす can be obtained by changing the final せる of
the regular causative form to す: 手伝わせる (causative form) →
手伝わす (shortened causative form).

5. 踏んだり蹴ったり lit. "being trod on and kicked"
This is an idiomatic expression used when a person encounters
one predicament after another.

6. 寄ってみようか lit. "Shall we stop by (to see how she's doing)?"
This is the Vte + みる pattern (Note 3, p. 95) in the volitional
form, followed by か. It expresses a suggestion.

7. 買わされちゃった "was made to buy …"
買わされちゃった is a contraction of 買わされてしまった. In this
case, Vte + しまう conveys not only completion of an action
but also regret about the result.

C **A professor talks with one of his students about the predicament he and his American guest experienced on a re-
cent fishing trip.**

72

学生　週末はお天気が悪かったですね。釣り場で雨に降

　　　られましたか。

教授　降られたよ。どしゃ降りだった。ホテルに走りこ

　　　んで、それから一歩も外に出られなかった。

学生　じゃあ、ホテルの部屋に閉じ込められていらっ

しゃったんですね。

教授　そう。その上、隣の部屋に騒がれて、全くまいったよ。

学生　せっかくアメリカのお客様をお連れになったのに

残念でございましたね。

教授　彼もがっかりしていたよ。でも次の機会を楽しみ

にしているんだ。

Student	The weather was terrible over the weekend. Were you rained on at your fishing spot?
Professor	We got rained on. It was a downpour. We rushed into the hotel, and we couldn't take another step outside after that.
Student	Then you were shut up in your hotel room?
Professor	That's right. Moreover, (the people in) the room next door made a lot of noise, so I got totally worn out (by the end of it).
Student	How regrettable (that things turned out like that)—and to think you brought an American guest with you.
Professor	He, too, was disappointed. But we are looking forward to the next opportunity.

！ Notes

1. 雨に降られました "be rained on"
降られる is the passive form of the intransitive verb 降る (of

rain: fall). In this case the passive is used to express suffering or discomfiture on the speaker's part that is caused by someone else's actions or something's (nature's) happenings.

2. 閉じ込められていらっしゃった "**you were shut up**"
閉じ込められていらっしゃった is the honorific equivalent of 閉じ込められていた, which consists of 閉じ込める (shut up) in the passive form.

3. 騒がれて "**they made a lot of noise (to my annoyance)**"
騒がれる, the passive form of the intransitive verb 騒ぐ (make noise), is used to express suffering on the speaker's part.

4. まいった "**got exhausted**"
まいった is the past tense of the special humble verb まいる (go, come) and is used here to express dismay or fatigue. In other cases まいった can express defeat.

5. せっかく "**kindly**," "**with great effort**"
せっかく is an adverb that expresses the speaker's regret over what he views as a wasted opportunity or effort.

✎ Practice

What would you say in the following situations? Hint: In some cases you will need to use passive, causative, or causative-passive forms.

1. You want to tell your new classmate that everybody respects (尊敬する) Professor Takagi (lit. that Professor Takagi is respected by everybody).

2. You want to tell your coworker that Ms. Kitano looks sad (悲しい) because her mother passed away (亡くなる).

3. You want to ask someone if he got rained on at the golf course (ゴルフ場).

4. You want to tell your husband that everybody hates (嫌う) the section chief (lit. he is hated) because he forces the employees (社員) to work overtime (残業する).

5. You want to ask your classmate whether the teacher scolded (叱る) Jim (lit. whether he got scolded) because he forgot (忘れる) his homework.

6. You want to tell your neighbor that the doctor ordered your husband (lit. that your husband was ordered by the doctor) to quit smoking.

7. You want to tell your sister that a cat ate the fish that Dad caught (釣る) (lit. that the fish Dad caught was eaten by a cat).

APPENDIXES

A. Answers to the Practice Questions

Note: In many cases there is more than one correct answer, and not all correct answers are listed.

Lesson 1

1. 父　2. どなた　3. です　4. です / でございます　5. でございます, どちら様

Lesson 2

1. ✕　2. ◯　3. ✕　4. ✕　5. ◯

Lesson 3

1. 毎朝8時に出勤されます / ご出勤になります
2. 何時にお出かけになりますか / 出かけられますか
3. 今日のミーティングは何時からですか
4. 先週ヨーロッパから帰られました / お帰りになりました
5. 水曜日までにいらっしゃいます / おいでになります

Lesson 4

1. 一番近いバス停はどこですか。　　2. ここはどこですか。　3. 孝はどこ?
4. 佐々木先生はどちらですか。 / 佐々木先生はどちらにいらっしゃいますか。
5. この近くにパン屋はありますか。

Lesson 5

1. 「トム、昨日の試験はどうだった?」「そんなに難しくなかったよ」
2. 「あのスーパーの (お) 野菜は新鮮で安いですね」「ええ、そうですね」
3. 「私の新しいピアノの先生は性格が優しいし、親切なの」「よかったわねえ!」
4. 「社長、ご旅行はお楽しみになりましたか」「最高だったな / 申し分なかったよ」
5. 「和夫、お帰りなさい。今日のお弁当、どうだった? おいしかった?」「うん、おいしかったよ」

Lesson 6

1. あのジャケットはいくらですか。
2. リンダ (さん)、おすしとてんぷらと、どっち (のほう) が好き?
3. 今日のテストは昨日のより易しかったです。
4. 3人の新入社員の中で、だれが一番有能かな。
5. 九州は東京と同じくらい暑うございましたが、東京ほど蒸し暑く (は) ございませんでした。

190

Lesson 7

1. 英語で話したり日本語で話したりなさいます
2. 坂田さんにどこで会われますか / 坂田さんにどちらで会われますか / 坂田さんにどこでお会いになりますか / 坂田さんにどちらでお会いになりますか
3. この素敵なバッグ、どこで買ったの
4. 日本酒も洋酒も飲みます
5. 昨日、美術館で何をごらんになりましたか

Lesson 8

1. 結婚しています / 結婚しております
2. 古典文学を研究しています / 古典文学を研究しております
3. このドアは開けてあるのですか
4. 地下鉄で会社に通っていらっしゃいます
5. このデータは直してありますか

Lesson 9

1. したんだろう? → なさったのでしょう?
2. 故障したんで → 故障したので, 遅れたんだ → 遅れたんです, すまん → 申し訳ございません
3. 出張した → 出張された, 出席されたんです → 出席したんです
4. 田中さん夫婦 → 田中さんご夫婦, 滞在した → 滞在された, 私達ご夫婦 → 私達夫婦, 滞在されたんです → 滞在したんです
5. 帰りましたか → 帰られましたか / お帰りになりましたか, 来られた → 来た, 話しております → 話していらっしゃいます

Lesson 10

A. 1. うん、行こう, いや、今晩はだめだよ
2. ええ、そうしましょう, そうですねえ、帰りはちょっと……
3. ええ、よろこんで, ありがとう、でもその日はちょっと……
B. 1. 部屋を片付けたらどう?
2. 今、返事しないほうがいいですよ。
3. 山岸さんをゴルフにお招きになったらどうでしょうか。

Lesson 11

1. 会議が始まるまでにデータを調べてください。
2. ここに駐車しないでいただけませんか。
3. 宿題を済ませてから遊びなさい。
4. その部屋には入らないでいただけますか。

5. その写真を見せて。

Lesson 12

1. 宏君、泳げるの？
2. 日本語を読むのは易しいですが、書くのは難しいです。 / 日本語を読むことは易しいですが、書くことは難しいです。
3. サム、日本人の友達に英語を教えること（が）できる？
4. 先生、この文を訳すことができません。
5. 課長、部長は中国語を話すことがお得意ですか。
6. 友子、うちの子、歩くようになったのよ。
7. 父は車を運転することができません。
8. すき焼きを作ることがおできになりますか。
9. ホールでコンサートのチケット、買うことできる？ / ホールでコンサートのチケット、買える？

Lesson 13

1. ほしがっています 2. 会いたいです 3. ほしいです, ほしがっています
4. 読んでほしいです 5. 見たがっていらっしゃいます 6. いらないよ, 連れてって
7. 訳していただきたいです

Lesson 14

A. 1. 晩ご飯までに帰るつもりだよ。(male) / 晩ご飯までに帰るつもりよ。(female)
2. 大学へ行かないつもりです。
3. 外車を買うことにしたよ。(male/female) / 外車を買うことにしたの。(female)
4. 機会があったら富士山に登るつもりです。
5. 雪が降れば運転しないつもりです。

B. 1. コーヒーと紅茶と、どちらになさいますか。
2. 大学を出たらどうするつもり？ (male/female) / 大学を出たらどうするつもりだ？ (male)
3. ご旅行にお子さんを連れていらっしゃるおつもりですか。 / ご旅行にお子さんをお連れになるおつもりですか。
4. 日本人の(お)友達と京都を見物するつもりですか。
5. 夏休みの間どこで働くつもり？ (male/female) / 夏休みの間どこで働くつもりだ？ (male)

Lesson 15

1. この小包を開けてもよろしいでしょうか。 / この小包を開けてもよろしゅうございますか。

2. えんぴつで書いてはいけません。
3. トムと一緒にキャンプに行ってもいい?
4. 水曜日までに本を図書館に返さなければなりません。
5. お姉さんのネックレス、借りていい?
6. 明日、仕事に来なくてもよろしいでしょうか。
7. 庭に自転車を置いてはだめよ。(female) / 庭に自転車を置いてはだめだよ。(male)
8. 料金は今お支払いにならなくても、よろしゅうございます。

Lesson 16

1. 東京の高校で英語を教えたことがございます。
2. 子供の時、ドイツに住んでいたことがあるの(よ)。
3. まださしみを食べたことがないんだよ。
4. 一人で夕食を食べに行くことはめったにないわ。
5. うちの主人は時々バーで友達と飲むことがあるんです。
6. まだ原博士のお宅にうかがったことはございません。
7. すもうはテレビでしか見たことがありません。
8. 僕、時々、日本人の友達と日本語で話すことがあるんだ。

Lesson 17

1. 行けないかもしれないわ　2. あったようです　3. なさるはずです
4. 辞めるはずがない(よ)　(male/female) / はずがないわ(よ)　(female)
5. だろう, にちがいない(よ)
6. 書いていらっしゃる / お書きになっているそうです　7. らしい, でしょう(ね)

Lesson 18

1. やった　2. いただき　3. あげて, くれる　4. さし上げ　5. いただき
6. もらい　7. ください　8. あげ / やり

Lesson 19

1. 高木先生はみんなに尊敬されている(よ)。(male/female) / 尊敬されていらっしゃるわ。(female)
2. 北野さんはお母様が亡くなったので、悲しそうです。
3. ゴルフ場で雨に降られましたか。
4. 課長は社員に残業させるから、みんなに嫌われて(い)るわ。
5. ジムは宿題を忘れたから、先生に叱られたの?
6. 主人は(お)医者(さん)にタバコを止めさせられたんです。
7. お父さんが釣った魚、猫に食べられちゃったよ。(male/female) / お父さんが釣った魚、猫に食べられちゃったわ。(female)

B. Verb Conjugation Chart

	Dictionary	Polite/-Masu	-Masu Stem	-Te	-Ta/Past	Negative	Negative Past
Reg. I	言う	言います	言い	言って	言った	言わない	言わなかった
	書く	書きます	書き	書いて	書いた	書かない	書かなかった
	行く	行きます	行き	行って	行った	行かない	行かなかった
	話す	話します	話し	話して	話した	話さない	話さなかった
	待つ	待ちます	待ち	待って	待った	待たない	待たなかった
	死ぬ	死にます	死に	死んで	死んだ	死なない	死ななかった
	遊ぶ	遊びます	遊び	遊んで	遊んだ	遊ばない	遊ばなかった
	飲む	飲みます	飲み	飲んで	飲んだ	飲まない	飲まなかった
	帰る	帰ります	帰り	帰って	帰った	帰らない	帰らなかった
	ある	あります	あり	あって	あった	ない	なかった
	なさる	なさいます	なさい	なさって	なさった	なさらない	なさらなかった
Reg. II	いる	います	い	いて	いた	いない	いなかった
	着る	着ます	着	着て	着た	着ない	着なかった
	食べる	食べます	食べ	食べて	食べた	食べない	食べなかった
Irreg.	来る	来ます	来	来て	来た	来ない	来なかった
	する	します	し	して	した	しない	しなかった

Notes

1. Irregularities are highlighted gray. Forms in parentheses are rarely, if ever, used.
2. In written or highly formal spoken Japanese, the -masu stem is used, like the -te form, to join two sentences together with the meaning "and." The only exception is いる (be), which becomes おり (not い) when used as a conjunctive.

Passive	Causative	Causative-Passive	Imperative	-Ba Conditional	Potential	Volitional
言われる	言わせる 言わす	言わせられる 言わされる	言え	言えば	言える	言おう
書かれる	書かせる 書かす	書かせられる 書かされる	書け	書けば	書ける	書こう
行かれる	行かせる 行かす	行かせられる 行かされる	行け	行けば	行ける	行こう
話される	話させる 話さす	話させられる —	話せ	話せば	話せる	話そう
待たれる	待たせる 待たす	待たせられる 待たされる	待て	待てば	待てる	待とう
死なれる	死なせる 死なす	— 	死ね	死ねば	死ねる	死のう
遊ばれる	遊ばせる 遊ばす	遊ばせられる 遊ばされる	遊べ	遊べば	遊べる	遊ぼう
飲まれる	飲ませる 飲ます	飲ませられる 飲まされる	飲め	飲めば	飲める	飲もう
帰られる	帰らせる 帰らす	帰らせられる 帰らされる	帰れ	帰れば	帰れる	帰ろう
— —	— —	— —	(あれ)	あれば	—	(あろう)
— —	— —	— —	なさい	なされば	—	(なさろう)
いられる	いさせる いさす	いさせられる —	いろ	いれば	いられる	いよう
着られる	着させる 着さす	着させられる 	着ろ	着れば	着られる	着よう
食べられる	食べさせる 食べさす	食べさせられる 	食べろ	食べれば	食べられる	食べよう
来られる	来させる 来さす	来させられる 	来い	来れば	来られる	来よう
される	させる —	させられる —	しろ／せよ	すれば	できる	しよう

3. Besides the -ba conditional, there are two others: (1) the -tara conditional, obtained by adding ら to the -ta form of the verb, and (2) the nara conditional, formed by adding なら to the dictionary form.
4. なさる is honorific for する, but people do not use the imperative form なさい to command social superiors to do something.

C. Adjective Inflection Chart

	Prenominal	Polite/-Desu	Plain/-Da	Stem	Adverbial	-Te
I-adj.	いい	いいです	いい	よ	よく	よくて
	寒（さむ）い	寒（さむ）いです	寒（さむ）い	寒（さむ）	寒（さむ）く	寒（さむ）くて
Na-adj.	元気（げんき）な	元気（げんき）です	元気（げんき）だ	元気（げんき）	元気（げんき）に	元気（げんき）で
Irreg.	同（おな）じ	同（おな）じです	同（おな）じだ	同（おな）じ	同（おな）じに / 同（おな）じく	同（おな）じで

Notes

1. Irregularities are highlighted gray.
2. Dictionaries vary as to how they list na-adjectives, with some listing them with な and some without. The prenominal form is the form the adjective takes when it modifies (comes before) a noun, pronoun, or other substantive.
3. As with verbs, there are also -tara and nara conditional forms.
4. よ is the stem of いい, which is a more casual form of よい. But note that before そう in the pattern Adj stem + そうだ, よ becomes よさ, e.g. よさそうだ.
5. 同じ is irregular in that it has some characteristics of a na-adjective and others of an i-adjective. The usage of 同じく is limited.

-Ta/Past	Negative	Negative Past	-Ba Conditional
よかった	よくない	よくなかった	よければ
寒かった	寒くない	寒くなかった	寒ければ
元気だった	元気ではない 元気じゃない	元気ではなかった 元気じゃなかった	元気であれば
同じだった	同じではない 同じじゃない	同じではなかった 同じじゃなかった	同じであれば

References

Drohan, Francis G. *A Handbook of Japanese Usage*. Rutland: Charles E. Tuttle, 1991.

Iori, Isao, Shino Takanashi, Kumiko Nakanishi, and Toshihiro Yamada. *Shokyū o oshieru hito no tame no Nihongo bunpō handobukku*. Tokyo: 3A, 2000.

———. *Chūjōkyū o oshieru hito no tame no Nihongo bunpō handobukku*. Tokyo: 3A, 2001.

Japan Foundation and the Association of International Education, Japan. *Japanese Language Proficiency Test: Test Content Specifications (Revised Edition)*. Tokyo: Bonjinsha, 2002.

Kamiya, Taeko. *The Handbook of Japanese Adjectives and Adverbs*. Tokyo: Kodansha International, 2002.

———. *The Handbook of Japanese Verbs*. Tokyo: Kodansha International, 2001.

———. *Japanese Sentence Patterns for Effective Communication*. Tokyo: Kodansha International, 2005.

Makino, Seiichi and Michio Tsutsui. *A Dictionary of Basic Japanese Grammar*. Tokyo: Japan Times, 1989.

———. *A Dictionary of Intermediate Japanese Grammar*. Tokyo: Japan Times, 1995.

McClain, Yoko Matsuoka. *Handbook of Modern Japanese Grammar*. Tokyo: Hokuseido, 1981.

Sunakawa, Yuriko, Satoshi Komada, Mitsuko Shimoda, Mutsumi Suzuki, Sayo Tsutsui, Akiko Hasunuma, Andrej Bekes, and Junko Morimoto. *Kyoshi to gakushūsha no tame no Nihongo bunkei jiten*. Tokyo: Kuroshio, 1998.

（英文版）状況別の日本語会話表現集
Japanese for All Occasions

2010 年 12 月 24 月　第 1 刷発行

著　者　　神谷妙子
朗　読　　松永玲子／中島愛子／大根田良樹／澤田育子／
　　　　　竹田高利／西ノ園達大／黒川 樹
挿　画　　早川 修
発行者　　廣田浩二
発行所　　講談社インターショナル株式会社
　　　　　〒112-8652　東京都文京区音羽 1-17-14
　　　　　電話　03-3944-6493（編集部）
　　　　　　　　03-3944-6492（マーケティング部・業務部）
　　　　　ホームページ　www.kodansha-intl.com
印刷・製本所　　大日本印刷株式会社